THE
LAST
MEN

THE
LAST
MEN

LIBERALISM
AND THE DEATH
OF MASCULINITY

DR. CHARLES
CORNISH-DALE
THE RAW EGG NATIONALIST

Since 1947
REGNERY
An Imprint of Skyhorse Publishing, Inc.

Regnery books may be purchased in bulk at special discounts for sales promotion, corporate gifts, fund-raising, or educational purposes. Special editions can also be created to specifications. For details, contact the Special Sales Department, Regnery, 307 West 36th Street, 11th Floor, New York, NY 10018 or info@skyhorsepublishing.com.

Regnery® is an imprint of Skyhorse Publishing, Inc.®, a Delaware corporation.

Visit our website at www.regnery.com.
Please follow our publisher Tony Lyons on Instagram @tonylyonsisuncertain.

10 9 8 7 6 5 4 3 2 1

Library of Congress Cataloging-in-Publication Data is available on file.

Cover design by Kai Texel
Cover photograph of *Hercules and the Nemean Lion*, by Roman Anton Boos. Image taken by Wilfredor

Print ISBN: 978-1-5107-8678-3
eBook ISBN: 978-1-5107-8679-0

Printed in the United States of America

Contents

Man on the Edge

THIS IS a book about masculinity and its decline in the modern era. Here I outline the scale of the problem, the causes, and some solutions to it, individual and collective. This problem will, I think, shock you and may even scare you, especially when I tell you about the harmful effects of so-called endocrine-disrupting chemicals, which can affect pretty much every single process in the body by mimicking the effects of natural hormones such as estrogen. These chemicals can make you fat and infertile, and they can give you cancer, and what's worse—they're everywhere. But it's always my intention when I write about our current health crisis to offer simple, practical solutions. Yes, the problem is bad—very bad—but there are things you, as a man, can do about it, and things women can do, too. Lifestyle alterations like buying organic food or even cultivating your own can hugely reduce the burden of exposure to chemicals like pesticides, benefitting you and your loved ones.

But there are aspects of this problem that are, as far as I'm concerned, insoluble under our current political dispensation. I don't just mean left or right, either, although I think the left generally makes things far, far worse for men than the right does. I'm talking about the broader liberal democratic system within which all parties, and within which we, exist.

Unlike so many books on the problem (such as Richard Reeves's bestseller *Of Boys and Men*[1]), this book will not focus on factors like the growth of feminism, equality in the workplace, and a hostile, largely female-led media and academy that trade in ridiculous notions like "toxic masculinity" and villainize boys and men when they pursue their inborn masculine impulses. These considerations matter, of course, and will be touched on and discussed at various points, but they are surface-level manifestations of a deeper problem. I'm not going to suggest we need a male-advocacy movement or a different kind of equality in the workplace or life. Being nicer to men at work and valuing their contribution as much as the contributions of the girlbosses in HR is not the solution for anything, not really. It's obvious to me that men and women are different and that treating them the same and expecting the same from them is a recipe for disaster—and should have been anticipated as such by those who pushed it upon us.

Men at the End of History

THE DEEPER problem is biological, and it tracks with a long-term development in Western political, and now global, life. I believe the most convenient and illuminating way to approach this is through Francis Fukuyama's notion, much misunderstood, of the "End of History." Fukuyama is generally presented as being liberal hubris incarnate, a man who actually thought time had come to a standstill with the Western liberal victory over communism and the fall of the Soviet Union. Fukuyama may, in the three decades since the publication of his book *The End of History and the Last Man*,[2] have become that caricature, but the book itself repays a closer reading—or an *actual* reading, since most people who think themselves experts on the subject appear not to have opened the book at all.

Yes, Fukuyama was talking in historical terms about the evolution of political systems and the final triumph of liberalism, but what he offers is a searing Nietzschean critique of the liberal end-state in which man is reduced to a mere passive consumer, human cattle, a kind of satisfied dolt. This is the "Last Man" of the title. In particular, this Last Man is unable to find proper outlets for his *thymos*, a term Fukuyama borrows from the ancient Greeks to describe the thrusting, self-assertive desires that make men *men*, that push them to seek distinction over one another and to establish their will. The historical triumph of liberalism is the banishment of *thymos* from politics and life. And *thymos*, as far as I'm concerned, is a byword for testosterone, the master male hormone.

In a fundamental sense then, this is a book about the hormonal basis of political systems, something you don't often see.

Our Hormonal Democracy

SO, I'M going to pick up Fukuyama's critique of modern liberal democracy and reinterpret it in hormonal terms. I'll focus on two aspects of modern life that are reinforcing and exacerbating this new hormonal politics and are seemingly unavoidable aspects of how we live today: exposure to endocrine disruptors, and poor diet. During the 2024 election campaign, Robert F. Kennedy Jr. identified endocrine disruptors and processed food as key causes of America's chronic disease crisis as he sought to launch a presidential commission into the health of the nation. Endocrine disruptors and bad diet were also central to the Tucker Carlson documentary *The End of Men*,[3] which I starred in alongside Kennedy back in 2022.

I won't exhaust all the causes of masculine decline here— I'd need much more space to do that—but I will address what I consider to be the fundamental causes, which have also received far less attention than they should have.

Addressing these causes on an individual and national level would transform health and politics. But we would still face a difficult, unsettling question: Is it possible to be men *fully* in a liberal democracy? If not, and we want to be, what then?

CHAPTER 1

How the End of History Became the End of Men

"When people first grasp the extent to which biology has something to do with behavior, even subtle, complex, human behavior, there is often an initial evangelical enthusiasm for the convert, a massive placing of faith in the biological components of the story. And this enthusiasm is typically of a fairly reductive type—because of physics envy, because reductionism is so impressive, because it would be so nice if there were a single gene or hormone or neurotransmitter or part of the brain that was *it*, the cause, the explanation of everything. And the trouble with testosterone is that people tend to think this way in an arena that really matters."

—ROBERT SAPOLSKY, *The Trouble with Testosterone*

"Man's genital concentration is a reduction but also an intensification. He is a victim of unruly ups and downs. Male sexuality is inherently manic-depressive. Estrogen tranquilizes, but androgen agitates. Men are in a constant state of sexual anxiety, living on the pins and needles of their hormones. In sex, as in life, they are driven *beyond*—beyond the self, beyond the body. Even in the womb, this rule applies. Every fetus becomes female unless it is steeped in male hormone, produced by a signal from the testes. Before birth, therefore, a male is already beyond the female. But to be beyond is to be exiled from the center of life. Men know they are sexual exiles. They wander the earth seeking satisfaction, craving and despising, never content. There is nothing in that anguished motion for women to envy."

—CAMILLE PAGLIA, *Sexual Personae*

—◆◆—

FRANCIS FUKUYAMA'S 1989 essay "The End of History," and the book it spawned three years later, is remembered as a paean to the triumph of liberal capitalism at the end of the Cold War. In Fukuyama's own words, with the fall of Communism in Europe, mankind had reached, "not just the end of the Cold War, or the passing of a particular period of post-war history, but the end of history as such: that is, the end point of mankind's ideological evolution, and the universalization of Western liberal democracy as the final form of human government."[4]

To many after September 11, the Global War on Terror, the rise of China and the Migrant Crisis of 2015, and with the "Climate Crisis" supposedly about to make large swathes of the planet literally uninhabitable for human life, Fukuyama's pronouncement of the End of History was premature, to say the least.

Big things are very much still happening.

Of course, if you've taken the time to read Fukuyama, you'll know he wasn't saying that history—i.e., the onward progression of time and events—had ceased. Nobody, not even a Harvard political scientist, could be that dumb. Rather, Fukuyama believed the evolution of social and political forms—a process which, like Marx and Hegel, he saw as developing in a linear fashion by means of contradictions and clashes—had finally come to an end. By defeating communism, liberal capitalist democracy had shown once and for all its superiority as a way of ordering life. Based on what we know about politics, economics, and ethics—and about man himself—nothing better could ever come along. And although there might be regressions, moments when the totalitarian impulses of the mid-20th century returned, these would always prove temporary. Liberal capitalist democracy would win again.

Always.

In Search of the Last Men

THE BASICS of Fukuyama's thesis are apt to be misrepresented, and Fukuyama himself is often made to serve as a straw man for the Western liberal elite and its monumental hubris, but other parts of his thesis are missed altogether. The title of his book is popularly known as *The End of History*. In fact, the full title is *The End of History and the Last Man*. This omission from the general consciousness is telling. Because not only is the book a proclamation of victory, it is also a warning—a warning that takes up the final fifth of the book. A warning about the Last Man.

Who or what is this Last Man?

The Last Man is a creature first identified in the late 19th century by the German philosopher Friedrich Nietzsche. Here's what Fukuyama has to say about this creature:

> Nietzsche's Last Man was, in essence, the victorious slave. [Nietzsche] fully agreed with Hegel that Christianity was a slave ideology, and that democracy represented a secularized form of Christianity. The equality of all men before the law was a realization of the Christian ideal of the equality of all believers in the Kingdom of Heaven. But the Christian belief

in the equality of men before God was nothing more than a prejudice, a prejudice born out of the resentment of the weak against those who were stronger than they were. The Christian religion originated in the realization that the weak could overcome the strong when they banded together in a herd, using the weapons of guilt and conscience. In modern times this prejudice had become widespread and irresistible, not because it had been revealed as true, but because of the greater numbers of weak people.[5]

Fukuyama goes on to argue that instead of being a "synthesis of the morality of the master and the morality of the slave, as Hegel had believed, to Nietzsche the liberal democratic state was slave morality through and through."

For Nietzsche, it represented an unconditional victory of the slave. The master's freedom and satisfaction were nowhere preserved, for no one really *ruled* in a democratic society. The typical citizen of a liberal democracy was that individual who, schooled by Hobbes and Locke, gave up prideful belief in his or her own superior worth in favor of comfortable self-preservation. For Nietzsche, democratic man was composed entirely of desire and reason, clever at finding new ways to satisfy a host of petty wants through the calculation of long-term self-interest. But he was completely lacking in any *megalothymia*, content with his happiness and unable to feel any sense of shame in himself for being unable to rise above those wants.[6]

In simple terms, the Last Man is what you get at the End of History, when there's no longer anything particularly important worth living for. When the great ethical, economic and political questions have all been settled, what higher purposes exist for men to strive towards? The answer is: none. Life becomes dull not through any individual defect but on a metaphysical level.

The Changing Place of Thymos

MEGALOTHYMIA, A Greek word, is key here. *Thymos*, according to the Greeks, was the part of an individual's soul that desires recognition or dignity. The word could be translated as something approximating "spiritedness" or "warm-bloodedness." It's an attribute all men possess and can develop. Fukuyama explains how Plato "compares a man with thymos to a noble dog who is capable of great courage and anger fighting strangers in defense of his own city."[7] *Thymos* can be equated, in some sense, with what might today be called "self-esteem." As Fukuyama puts it, "*Thymos* is something like an innate sense of justice: people believe that they have a certain worth, and when other people act as though they are worthless—when they do not *recognize* their worth at its correct value—then they become angry."[8]

Thymos, then, is intimately tied to a person's place in the social order, to his sense of self-worth (which must be reflected in others), and to his desire, ultimately, to assert his claim to these things. Fukuyama generally describes *thymos* as the "desire for recognition."

The Greeks believed *thymos* came in various forms. There was *isothymia*, a desire to be acknowledged as equal to everybody else, which can be seen as the central impulse at the heart of the Christian and democratic ideals. Then there was *megalothymia*, which is the desire to seek distinction above others, in opposition to *isothymia*.

In the liberal-democratic end-state, where all men have been decided, at last, to be equal, *isothymia* is satisfied, but *megalothymia* is not and cannot be. Ever. And that's not good.

In *Civilization and Its Discontents*, Sigmund Freud cautioned that when an entire population has unfulfilled or even deliberately suppressed desires, turmoil will follow. This is the crux of Fukuyama's warning about the End of History: man's nature cannot be denied. While it's entirely possible that man will be happy now as one among many billions of equals, each pursuing his own limited goals like making money, buying things, having sex, and going on holidays, it's equally possible that man—or rather *some* men—will rebel in the name of satisfying their desire to be different. To be better. What we might see instead of a future of cattle-like dolts enjoying an easy contentment is "immense wars of the spirit"—and Fukuyama means, quite literally, *wars*—with wild men letting loose and painting the world red again in the name of personal glory and some higher purpose whatever that might be—that is, anything other than endless, monotonous peace and sex and commerce.

This is the scenario dramatized by the French writer Michel Houellebecq in his second novel *Platform*,[9] where a self-satisfied French sex tourist, having reconciled himself to a life of hedonism on the beaches of Thailand, is caught up in a violent Islamic terrorist attack that kills his partner and eventually drives him to suicide.

Isothymia, say hello to your old friend *megalothymia*!

Not with a Bang but a Whimper?

SO WHAT began as a supposedly ringing and uncomplicated endorsement of liberal democratic capitalism by Fukuyama has ended with a dire warning about the degeneration of man in a social prison of his own making and the desperate attempts he might make to free himself from it at any cost. Whatever Fukuyama's original intention, *The End of History* offers one of the most devastating criticisms not only of the democratic form but of the forces that are making life hostile on a planetary scale to the human spirit. Although I don't agree that liberal democratic capitalism is the end stage of man's social and political development, I do agree the "unipolar moment" that followed the fall of communism in Europe was a hollow victory, and that, so long as liberalism is in the ascendant, man—and specifically *men*—are going to continue to suffer from a profound crisis of meaning and purpose.

In certain respects, however, I think Fukuyama's assessment of man's degeneration at the End of History is too optimistic. Yes, you read that right: *too* optimistic. Because Fukuyama saw *thymos* as a fixed quantity, something men would retain even in the face of a social and political system that was utterly hostile to the expression of *thymos* as individual distinction.

The reality is that *thymos* is not a fixed quantity. *Thymos* can be drained—by bad food, by bad lifestyles, by bad chemicals—and that's precisely what is happening now. Fukuyama's thesis can be extended beyond the political to the *biological* level.

The frustration of *thymos* in the modern world is not simply the frustration of liberal democracy. It's also a deeper biological decline working in tandem with liberal democracy and modernity, with capitalism and industry.

Testosterone as Thymos

YOU MAY wonder what such seemingly esoteric philosophical discussion has to do with the problems men face in their everyday physical, gritty, biological lives. A lot, actually.

Because *thymos* is, for all intents and purposes, testosterone. These physical and metaphysical problems go hand in hand. Rather than talking in terms of *thymos*—or rather than talking *solely* in terms of *thymos*—I'm going to explain what's happening to men by reference to the stunning decline in testosterone levels they've experienced in recent decades. Testosterone decline is something few conservatives or right-wingers have talked about until recently, but it's something that has implications that touch the fundamental issues we care about (or at least *should* care about).

Testosterone makes for a strong proxy for *thymos* because testosterone is what essentially makes men men. The kinds of behaviors that are associated with *thymos*, and with being a man more broadly, are clearly linked to levels of testosterone in the body. A man's testosterone levels may be the difference between a life of sex and success and a life spent rotting in a fetid basement, playing video games and eating chicken tenders heated up in the microwave by Mum. The Japanese *hikikomori*, extreme social recluses, have been shown to have lower levels of testosterone than normal men, for example. Indeed, reams of scientific studies show that testosterone levels are correlated with everything from attractiveness to assertiveness, and that men who lack testosterone are more likely to be overweight, depressed, anxious, unmotivated, and infertile. What's more, we can measure testosterone levels in men quite nicely, and in a way that simply isn't possible with an abstract concept like *thymos*. By looking at testosterone levels, we can be precise, and that's never a bad thing.

High-quality research, such as the Massachusetts Male Aging Study, featuring many thousands of men, reveals a precipitous decline in testosterone levels across the developed world from the U.S. to Scandinavia and Israel. Year on year, decade after decade, testosterone levels have been falling as part of a broader collapse in male fertility. Given the decline in sperm counts in recent decades, one expert has even suggested that within twenty-five years, it might be impossible for humans to reproduce by natural means at all.

What's causing this? One cause is a class of chemicals known as endocrine disruptors. Endocrine disruptors work by interfering with the body's hormonal system, particularly the crucial balance of the sex hormones testosterone and estrogen, which is responsible for determining whether we end up male or female—or something in between. Endocrine disruptors are everywhere—they're in the food, they're in the water, they're in the air, they're in personal-care products and soaps and perfumes—and as we're now discovering, they're having a terrifying effect on human health, not least of all gender and fertility. For the better part of a decade, Alex Jones has been mocked for his legendary "gay frogs" rant, and the claim that exposure to endocrine disruptors like the herbicide atrazine is causing gender-bending effects in amphibians and, by implication, humans as well. But the truth is, that claim was totally plausible when Jones made it in 2014, and we now have credible research that directly links endocrine disruptors to the explosion of transgenderism that's taken place in the last few decades. Endocrine disruptors are unraveling gender at the biological level.

You Are What You Eat

SO THAT'S one probable cause we'll be examining in detail. Another is changing diet. Over the last century and a half, diets in the Western world, and increasingly now in the non-Western world, have undergone as profound a change as any that has taken place in human history. In place of the kind of locally produced whole-food diets our ancestors ate for the longest period, we decided to substitute a new class of processed or ultra-processed food, made in factories using an increasing number of novel ingredients and additives, and packaged and sold to us from supermarket shelves with only convenience—and corporate profit—in mind. This dietary shift has been a disaster from the beginning. The work of the pioneering dentist Weston A. Price reveals the dramatic health effects of the very first processed foods (refined flour products, canned and tinned foods, sugar syrups) introduced to America and Europe around the turn of the twentieth century. Price called this "physical degeneration," and showed how traditional societies, by contrast, maintained "perfect health" by consuming nutrient-dense animal foods like organ meat and fatty cuts, dairy, butter and other fat products, seafood and shellfish, and eggs.

In the intervening decades since the publication of Price's *Nutrition and Physical Degeneration*,[10] our dependence on factory-produced food has only increased and continues to increase. The average toddler in the U.K. now derives around two-thirds of his daily calories from ultra-processed food, and the U.S. and other Western nations aren't far behind. Increasing consumption of processed food is linked to more or less every one of the prevailing chronic diseases of the modern age, from diabetes and obesity to Alzheimer's and autism. The physical degeneration is getting worse.

The Chemical Onslaught

TOXIC CHEMICALS and toxic food—these don't exhaust the causes of testosterone decline, but they're definitely among the most important. Toxic chemicals in particular have received far less attention than they deserve as causes of ill health. A big part of my work from the very beginning as the Raw Egg Nationalist has been to raise awareness of the extent to which exposure to chemicals like bisphenol A (BPA) and phthalates in everything from bottled water to deodorant and sunscreen is robbing us of our health, and I want to continue that awareness-raising here. Focusing on these two causes of bad health also aligns with the agenda of Robert F. Kennedy Jr., who, as head of the Department of Health and Human Services, has been tasked by President Trump to "Make America Healthy Again." During the presidential campaign and through his many decades of health advocacy, RFK Jr. has campaigned to clean up the environment, consumer products, and the food and water supply.

RFK Jr. was also one of the principal stars, along with me, of the 2022 Tucker Carlson documentary *The End of Men*, about the problem of testosterone decline, its causes, and its social and political implications. Later, we'll look at that documentary, including what the media response to it revealed about the place of masculinity in liberal politics today.

"Make America Healthy Again" couldn't have come a moment too soon. For so long, health and fitness have been considered as side-effects, distractions with little to no political bearing. Whether or not you choose to take care of your body, whether you choose to exercise and eat well or sit on your arse all day and eat processed food, has been seen as a matter of personal choice and nothing more. A personal choice, like whether you prefer early or later Fleetwood Mac. Or a whim of your upbringing, like whether you follow baseball or can't stand it. And yet, the massive burden of ill health on the government and the taxpayer is there for all to see. The national cost of obesity alone in the U.S. is estimated to be north of $200 billion a year.[11] Never mind that such an enormous amount, almost certainly an underestimate, could be better used to pay for all sorts of far more useful things—twenty border walls between the U.S. and Mexico, for example, or an enormous package of infrastructure renewal, or multiple manned flights to Mars. Never mind, people *must* be allowed to carry on eating themselves into chronic disease and a slow, lingering living death.

I've puzzled for a long time about why this absurd attitude to health emerged and why it persists in the face of so much evidence of its appalling immediate and knock-on effects. Obviously, it comes in part from the development of liberalism and its apparently "value-neutral" frame, which studiously discriminates against discrimination, but I also think it has as much to do with our long-standing dualist metaphysics, which posits an absolute separation between mind and body. This is a separation our ancestors and other cultures would have had great trouble understanding. The actual truth, as the ancient Greeks knew, is that man is an integrated whole, mind *and* body. Neither can exist in good health without the other existing in good health, too. This sentiment was nicely expressed by the great historian Thucydides, we're told: "The society that separates its scholars from its warriors will have its thinking done by cowards and its fighting by fools." We would do well to remember this.

Instead of retaining the desire and ability to exercise *megalothymia*, under our current conditions of massive prosperity, men are losing the desire and ability to do—well, just about anything. Look around you. Everywhere you turn, men, especially younger men, are overweight, depressed, disillusioned, and unmotivated. For a variety of reasons, some of which Fukuyama identified—including a lack of overarching meaning and worthwhile goals to strive for—men have ceased, in important respects, to be men. More and more young men are opting out of manhood, as it were,

13

and choosing a prolonged adolescence living in isolation from others and especially from the opposite sex. According to recent Pew Research Center polling, 63 percent of American men in their 20s are now single.[12] Sexlessness among young men tripled between 2008 and 2018.[13] While we hear plenty about the demoralizing and degrading influence of pornography and video games or of a liberal culture that is becoming more hostile to basic expressions of masculinity by the day, we hear much less about the biological and physical factors driving this descent into a kind of shadow existence for young men.

Jordan Peterson and the Weight of Masculinity

MASCULINE DECLINE—the "crisis of masculinity"—is a hot topic today. It's the subject that's launched a thousand books, podcasts, and self-help Twitter accounts run by Desi gurus with Roman statues as their profile pictures. The Jordan B. Peterson phenomenon is perhaps the best example of this. Peterson's emergence as a public intellectual and sage of self-help has generated an outpouring of emotion and interest from young men that borders on the religious. Peterson has been elevated to the level of a prophet simply because he offers leadership and example to young men who are so desperately, desperately in need of those things, whether because they come from one of an ever-increasing number of broken homes without a father or because they inhabit the position, by default, of a second-class citizen in a gynocratic, misandrist society that punishes them at every turn for wanting what young men have always wanted. Often it's both.

At times, Peterson is visibly overcome, unable to contain the huge weight of emotion and expectation that's placed on his shoulders. He periodically collapses into tears when discussing the plight of young men. He's often mocked for this, but the burden he carries and the scale of the problem are very real. Young men really are being left to swing in the wind.

Peterson has focused some of his attention on food and the role of a strict carnivore diet in solving his own serious physical and mental health problems. At the end of 2024, he sat on a congressional health panel with RFK Jr. to consider the role of diet and other factors in America's chronic disease crisis. Peterson hasn't yet taken the specific step of linking men's problems today to declining testosterone or making the connection with harmful chemicals and changing diet, but perhaps he will someday.

Richard Reeves's Non-Solution

PETERSON SEEMS on the right track, but Richard Reeves' *Of Boys and Men* is as good an example as any of the blind spots of the "crisis of masculinity" literature more broadly. The approach is to look at social and cultural factors only and either dismiss the biological or not mention it at all. In *Of Boys and Men*, Reeves dedicates just two pages of sustained discussion to testosterone, and only in order to dispel the notion that men are "ruled" by their hormones and forced to be aggressive as a result. "We are not slaves to our cells," Reeves writes—which is true.[14] We are not slaves to our cells: we *are* our cells. Big difference.

The approach seems naïve at best, and Reeves seems committed to a "reasonable" frame of reference that accepts that modern society, and especially the "gains" of modern feminism, should be maintained and, if anything, enlarged rather than rolled back or reversed altogether.

Reeves has plenty to say about what he calls the "male malaise" and how men have lost their "natural" place in the workforce and the family and are falling behind in education. The stats don't lie. Reeves believes the problems, fundamentally, are "structural." Men, says Reeves, have lost their place in society because of aggregate changes at the social and cultural level, which can simply be worked out by better social policies:

> Boys are falling behind at school and college because the educational system is structured in ways that put them at a disadvantage. Men are struggling in the labor market because of an economic shift away from traditionally male jobs. And fathers are dislocated because the cultural role of family provider has been hollowed out. The male malaise is not the result of a mass psychological breakdown but of deep structural challenges.[15]

Again, true. This isn't just an individual problem that can be solved by telling men to "man up."

The solution, Reeves tells us, is to change society to be more accommodating to men. For Reeves, it boils down to evening out the advantages that have accrued to women because of feminism. As the blurb on the back of the book says, "We now need . . . a positive vision of masculinity that is compatible with gender equality." We need to be nicer to men; we need to recognize that they have a contribution to make to society that is different from women but just as valid and useful. Men aren't just oppressors or rapists in the making.

They're not. Even so, this whole approach—and Reeves isn't the only advocate—strikes me as very wrong-headed. I don't mean that men shouldn't be valued far more than they are or that the solution to the problem doesn't involve far-reaching structural changes. Both are undoubtedly true.

But the idea that the crux of the matter lies in not treating men nicely enough is a fundamental misunderstanding of masculinity and the nature of the problem itself. Books like *Of Boys and Men* reveal that their male authors are incapable of grappling with the true nature of masculinity in a way that a woman like Camille Paglia is. Paglia's quote at the beginning of the chapter says far more in a few sentences about the listless, anguished nature of being a man, driven on by the throbbing, pulsing rhythms of testosterone, than hundreds of pages of Richard Reeves's anemic diagnosis and prescription. "Men know they are sexual exiles," Paglia says. "They wander the earth seeking satisfaction, craving and despising, never content. There is nothing in that anguished motion for women to envy."

Modern Life and the "Iron Prison"

REEVES AND his fellow travelers simply don't want to face the darker, more disturbing facts about the modern world and its "iron prison" for men, to borrow a phrase from Bronze Age Pervert and *Bronze Age Mindset*, his take on a modern Nietzschean philosophy.[16] Perhaps they can't.

The strength of Fukuyama's account, by contrast, even if it hasn't explicitly been couched as a contribution to the "crisis of masculinity" literature, is that it allows us to recognize not only that something is missing, something profound at the heart of liberal democracy, but that "something" is connected to the civilizational changes identified by philosophers like Friedrich Nietzsche, which go far, far beyond the enervating effects of DEI quotas at work and the ubiquity of sassy female leads in Netflix shows and movies.

In the final chapter, I'll make individual recommendations for how you, as a man, can start to reclaim your health. As I said in the preface, I don't intend to leave anyone in despair when I talk about endocrine disruptors or processed food or microplastics, as depressing as these subjects might be. There are things you *can* do, very simple things, to reduce your exposure to harmful substances and to boost natural processes within the body that will help to renew your health and maybe even transform your life. The scale of the problem is enormous—unparalleled even—but simple actions can make a huge difference. All my recommendations will be listed together in a handy appendix at the end, for ease of reference.

These recommendations also apply if you're a woman. The witch's brew of lifestyle factors like obesity and inactivity, coupled with our exposure to harmful chemicals of a kind and quantity that are without parallel in our history, affects women's well-being as much as men's and prevents women from realizing their potential for womanhood, including their most essential biological role, as bearers of children. The end of men is also the end of women.

But the question remains: What can we *really* do about masculinity under liberal democracy? Perhaps we can fix our individual and collective health—RFK Jr. is certainly attempting to do so, and I for one want him to succeed—but what then? If we restore *thymos* to men, their rightful inheritance, where do we go with a system that seems rigged to prevent its fullest expression?

CHAPTER 2

Enter the Men Without Chests

"In a sort of ghastly simplicity we remove the organ and demand the function. We make men without chests and expect of them virtue and enterprise. We laugh at honour and are shocked to find traitors in our midst. We castrate and bid the geldings be fruitful."

—C.S. LEWIS, *The Abolition of Man*

"A dozen millennia ago or so, an adventurous soul managed to lop off a surly bull's testicles and thus invented behavioral endocrinology. It is unclear from the historical records whether this individual received either grant or tenure as a result of this experiment, but it certainly generated an influential finding—something or other comes out of the testes that helps to make males such aggressive pains in the ass. That something or other is testosterone."

—ROBERT M. SAPOLSKY, *The Trouble with Testosterone*

— ♦♦♦ —

The Trouble with Testosterone Today

T HE MASSACHUSETTS Male Aging Study (MMAS), which began in the late 1980s, was a random-sample, population-based, cross-sectional observational study of 1,709 healthy men aged 40–70 years and living in the Boston area.[17] In simple terms, that means a random sample of men was taken from the local male population aged 40–70, and their health was monitored in a variety of different ways over a period of years. The male subjects were visited at home, where they filled in questionnaires, were measured physically (for example, their body-mass index was determined), and had blood samples taken, so that a number of different health markers could be measured. Initially, the study ran from 1987 to 1989, but then there were clinic-based follow-ups from 1995 to 1997 and 2002 to 2004.

The MMAS is generally considered to be a gold standard for observational studies. It uses a truly random sample of people from the community rather than a sample of people associated with a clinic or institution, which couldn't be considered random in the fullest sense. The sample size is large enough to allow estimation of the prevalence of rare phenomena, and to allow sub-group analysis—the breaking down of the subject population into smaller groups by particular traits—and adjustment for confounding variables (influences that might affect the validity of results). The study was multidisciplinary, incorporating hormonal, anthropometric, lifestyle, psychosocial, nutritional, and biomedical data. It's one of the only long-term studies of erectile dysfunction, and has provided important observational data on prostate cancer, diabetes, and cardiovascular disease. In short, this was an extremely well-designed, genuinely reliable observational study of male health. Gold standard, like I said.

The study also allowed long-term measurement and comparison of trends in hormonal function, particularly testosterone levels. Testosterone levels were measured as part of the blood sampling that took place throughout the study.

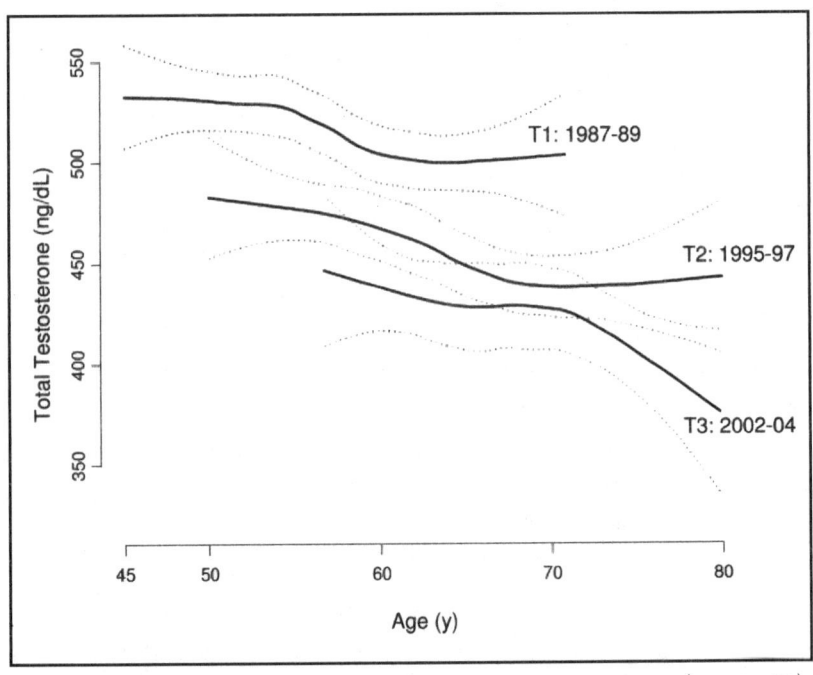

CRUDE MEAN TT CONCENTRATIONS, BY MMAS STUDY WAVE (T1, T2, T3) WITH CONFIDENCE BANDS (DOTTED LINES), THE JOURNAL OF CLINICAL ENDOCRINOLOGY & METABOLISM, 2007[18]

One of the important goals of the study was to document hormonal changes within individuals over time to see how testosterone levels change. It had been observed that testosterone levels generally decrease by 1–2 percent per year for a man once he reaches the age of about 30. The study would also allow comparison of trends in testosterone on a population level. Were levels increasing? Were they decreasing? Staying the same, perhaps?

In 2007, a detailed study of the testosterone data over the entire span of the MMAS was published.[19] The results were not good. "Alarming" would be the word.

> "We observe a substantial age-independent decline in T that does not appear to be attributable to observed changes in explanatory factors, including health and lifestyle characteristics such as smoking and obesity. The estimated population-level declines are greater in magnitude than the cross-sectional declines in T typically associated with age."[20]

Both total and bioavailable levels of testosterone—that's testosterone the body can actually use—declined spectacularly, year on year, with total decreases of over 20 percent in both types of testosterone in less than twenty years. One-fifth of total and bioavailable testosterone gone in less than a generation.

As the quotation indicates, the analysis showed that the drops could not simply be explained by factors like obesity or smoking—because the authors could isolate and control for these confounding variables. Something else was going on. The researchers couldn't say what, though:

> These results indicate that recent years have seen a substantial, and as yet unrecognized, age-independent population-level

decrease in T in American men, potentially attributable to birth cohort differences or to health or environmental effects not captured in observed data.[21]

A Civilization at Risk

RESEARCHERS IN Finland wanted to investigate whether a similar population-level decrease was taking place among Finnish men.[22] They believed it was unlikely since Finnish men score higher on various indexes of reproductive health—for example, semen quality, incidence of cryptorchidism (undescended testicles), and prostate cancer—than American men generally do. They looked at three large population samples of men aged 25–74, totaling twice the number of men in the MMAS, from surveys taken in 1972, 1977, and 2002. What they found was a testosterone decline every bit as vicious as among the men from the Boston area. Serum testosterone levels in men aged 60 to 69 decreased from 21.9 nmol/l, in men born between 1913 and 1922, to 13.8 nmol/l in men born 1942–51, a 37 percent decrease in roughly 30 years. The decreases remained significant even when adjustments were made for body-mass index and other factors. The study offered no explanation for the decrease in testosterone levels. Similar results were found in a study of 5,000 men from Denmark, which showed that men born in the 1960s had, on average, 14 percent less testosterone than men of the same age born in the 1920s.[23]

More recently, a study of testosterone levels among American adolescents (age fifteen to nineteen) and young adult men (twenty to thirty-nine) showed a large decline in testosterone levels between 1999 and 2016.[24] Again, after controlling for confounding factors such as BMI, physical activity, smoking and alcohol consumption, these decreases remained significant. As in the other studies, the decrease was around 1 percent a year across the study's timespan. The researchers note that 20 percent of all men aged 15 to 39 in the U.S. now have clinically low testosterone.

A study of Israeli men from 2020 showed a "highly significant independent decline in total testosterone in the first and second decades of the twenty-first century."[25] For men aged 21, for example, there was a decrease of about 10 percent in 10 years, from an average of 19.68 nmol/l in 2006–2009 to 17.76 nmol/l in 2016–2019.

This is bad—surely? Even if you don't know much about testosterone beyond the fact that men need it, you'd expect a decline in the hormone on this scale and across the developed world to have serious consequences, especially since the decline appears to be ongoing. A year-on-year decline of 1 percent in testosterone levels for the next 50 or 100 years would surely be a disaster.

You'd be right. But to understand what such an enormous decline might mean, first you need to understand what testosterone is and does, and that means, among other things, breaking a certain amount of conditioning about testosterone and aggression. Testosterone as the aggression hormone. Testosterone as the cause of fighting and wars. Testosterone as something we might be better off without. You see and hear it all the time today, whether you're reading a magazine or newspaper, or watching CNN's coverage of the Democratic National Convention. (We'll come back to that later.)

Some archaeologists have suggested, based on ancient skull evidence, that a drop in testosterone was necessary for the emergence of civilization itself. They found changes about 50,000 years ago to the skulls of modern humans—

especially reduced prominence of the brow ridge—that coincide with some of the earliest finds of tools.[26] Increased "craniofacial feminization," the researchers say, "reflects the evolution of enhanced social tolerance." If that was the case then, why not now, too? As society advances, do we even need testosterone?

Testosterone is involved in aggression and competition, absolutely, but the hormone does far, far more than that.

The Trouble with Testosterone: What We Know and How

TESTOSTERONE IS a hormone. Hormones are biological signaling molecules. They carry messages in physical form around the body. Hormones come in a wide variety of types, from eicosanoids and steroids to amino acids and proteins, and even gases, such as ethylene oxide (which makes plants ripen) and nitrous oxide (which causes blood vessels to dilate). All of these molecules encode messages that tell tissues within the body what to do. They do this by binding to receptor proteins in tissues, essentially flicking a switch that turns particular processes on or off.

Hormones largely exist within feedback loops, meaning the body constantly responds to changing levels of hormones and the processes they regulate to prevent dangerous fluctuations and disturbances, rather like a thermostat controls a heating system. Consider insulin, for example, the hormone responsible for reducing

TESTOSTERONE

blood-sugar levels. High blood-glucose levels cause the pancreas to secrete insulin, which then reduces glucose in the blood by promoting its absorption into the cells of the liver, fat, and skeletal muscle.

Testosterone, like estrogen and progesterone, is a specific sex hormone that governs sex-related aspects of the organism. Like estrogen, testosterone is a steroid hormone derived from cholesterol, which is produced by the body in the liver and consumed in the diet from animal foods. Most testosterone is produced in the Leydig cells of the male testes, and it works by binding to what are known as "androgen receptors" in the tissues, which turn on effects specific to androgenic hormones.

I've previously mentioned "total" and "free" testosterone. The total amount of testosterone is not necessarily the amount the body can use. Because testosterone is a lipophilic (i.e. fat- but not water-soluble) hormone, it must be transported through the blood by special carrier molecules. One of these carriers is called sex hormone-binding globulin (SHBG), and it binds to testosterone and makes it inactive. The portion of testosterone that is not bound to SHBG is the free testosterone, and it's this portion that can still bind to androgen receptors and have androgenic effects in the body. Bound testosterone cannot do this.

On average, men have about seven or eight times as much testosterone as women—although testosterone is important to female health and development, and estrogen is important to male health and development. A lot of men (especially on Twitter, when they're constantly reading health posts) get it into their heads that the best thing a man can do is totally rid his body of estrogen, but this couldn't be further from the truth. In men, estrogen is essential for bone development, erectile function, libido and reproductive health, the modulation of social behavior, body-fat storage and function, insulin sensitivity, and a number of other bodily processes. Men need estrogen—just far less of it than women do. And women need testosterone too—just far less of it than men do.[27]

Let's look at some of the specific things we know testosterone does. Testosterone governs the masculinization process that first occurs in boys in the womb and then resumes during adolescence. Processes directed and shaped by testosterone include the development of the penis and testes, deepening of the voice, the growth of facial and pubic hair, muscular and bone development, and libido and sperm production. The production of testosterone in men is regulated via the brain's pituitary gland, which sends signals to the testes to produce the hormone. Levels of the hormone, and of all hormones, are closely regulated within feedback loops. If testosterone levels are too high, the brain sends signals to the pituitary gland to reduce production, or the opposite if levels are low.

In addition to governing physical processes that are essential to the full expression of male sex, testosterone is involved in the regulation of mood and the expression of male behavior. Now you can be forgiven for believing that, in this regard, testosterone is simply the "aggressive" hormone, the hormone that makes men fight and kill and rape and do all the nasty retrograde things that need to be eliminated from society once and for all. We don't live in the Stone Age anymore, right? That's certainly how testosterone and its effects are portrayed in the media and pop science. The truth, unsurprisingly, is far more complicated and nuanced. Testosterone is not simply an "aggressive" or "anti-social" hormone. Increased levels of testosterone do not make a man reliably more dangerous. They might make him more formidable, a far worthier opponent for his fellow man and for life itself, but that's not the same thing, and we ought to know the difference.

The Feminized Monkey

ESTROGEN, THE "female" hormone that supposedly makes women the angelic nurturing creatures we all need and love, actually has a very important role to play in the modulation of aggression. This is demonstrated in a wonderful study I like to talk about as much as I can: "Increased aggressive behavior and decreased affiliative behavior in adult male monkeys after long-term consumption of diets rich in soy protein and isoflavones," in the journal *Hormones and Behavior*, from 2004.[28] By feeding male macaques a diet rich in soy compounds that mimic the hormone estrogen, scientists were able to make them simultaneously more aggressive and also more introverted and submissive:

> In the monkeys fed the higher amount of isoflavones, frequencies of intense aggressive (67 percent higher) and submissive (203 percent higher) behavior were elevated relative to monkeys fed the control diet . . . In addition, the proportion of time spent by these monkeys in physical contact with other monkeys was reduced by 68 percent, time spent in proximity to other monkeys was reduced 50 percent, and time spent alone was increased 30 percent . . . The results indicate that long-term consumption of a diet rich in soy isoflavones can have marked influences on patterns of aggressive and social behavior.[29]

I like to say that these feminized male monkeys became passive-aggressive "incel monkeys," an analogy that bears up surprisingly well in the human case when it comes to the effects of testosterone decline and feminization.

We'll get back to the specifics of what testosterone does, but let's consider for a moment the history of the hormone. It's been less than a hundred years since we've known what testosterone is, let alone its effects. That doesn't mean, though, that man had no idea of the masculinizing effects of testosterone. The connection between the testicles and manhood is one that was made a very, very long time ago. It's not hard to imagine primitive man making that connection simply on the basis of men having a penis and testicles and women not. Ergo, the penis and testicles make a man a man and not a woman. And given their appearance and structure—sacks—it wouldn't be too unreasonable to imagine the testes were carrying something valuable, too . . . Perhaps this brainwave reached man in some dimly lit cave at night or out on the savannah while hunting game. Who knows? But it seems plausible. My lizard brain told me so.

Discovering Hormones and Their Uses

ENOUGH SPECULATIVE history. The term "hormone" was coined by the scientist Ernest Starling in 1905, three years after discovering the first hormone, secretin, a digestive hormone released by the wall of the upper small intestine (duodenum) to regulate stomach acid secretion and pH levels. It would be another three decades—the mid-1930s—before testosterone was isolated and synthesized by multiple groups of scientists working independently of one another in laboratories in Germany, the Netherlands, and Switzerland.

Scientists had been searching excitedly to find a miraculous substance produced by the testes since the middle of the previous century when the German scientist Adolph Berthold castrated roosters and then re-grafted testicles on them. He noted how the roosters regained their aggression with the grafted testicles and concluded that the testicles must produce a substance that is responsible for this effect. Charles Édouard Brown-Sequard followed up on Berthold's experiments by injecting himself with blood from his testicular vein mixed with semen and "juice" from dog or guinea pig testes in equal parts. He claimed the mixture gave him massively increased strength, stamina, and energy. Brown-Sequard's paper, published in 1889, created a "whirlwind of experimentation" in the decades that followed.[30]

One of the joint discoverers of testosterone was Adolf Butenandt, who in 1931 isolated crystals of the androgenic (masculinizing) steroid androsterone from 15,000 liters of urine taken from German police officers. Those 15,000 liters of urine provided just 15mg of the hormone. Butenandt had also discovered the female hormone estrone—estrogen—in the same manner, using pregnant women's urine. Later, he would extract the hormone progesterone from pigs' ovaries.

Four years later in 1935, Ernst Laqueur and his team of scientists in Amsterdam extracted and then isolated 10mg of another hormone from 100kg of bull's testicles. They discovered the substance was a more potent androgenic than androsterone and named it "testosterone." That year, Butenandt and his team, and Ruzicka and Wettstein in Basel, published the first chemical synthesis of testosterone, and with it the modern age of male hormonal treatment can be said to have begun.

In the years and decades that followed, various new synthetic formulations of testosterone were created, beginning with intramuscular injections and oral formulations (which proved to be highly toxic), progressing to long-lasting subdermal pellets, suppositories and, more recently, gels that can be applied directly to the skin, which are now the standard treatment of choice for men with testosterone deficiencies. The discoveries of the 1930s also ushered in a new age of performance enhancement in sport and athletic competition, which has well and truly spilled over into the mainstream, with ordinary members of the public, even teenagers, using anabolic substances like never before to improve their appearance and performance. Estimates of anabolic steroid use vary widely, and base levels are likely to be significant underestimates. One study from 2014 reckoned that 6.4 percent of males worldwide have used anabolic steroids.[31] The same authors then produced a study of young men in Ghana that showed 66 percent of high-school athletes and 24 percent of recreational athletes have used them.[32]

Cutting Off Testosterone at the Source

ENDOCRINOLOGY—the study of hormones, and male hormones in particular—is much older than the 1930s. One way to consider the history of testosterone and its role in the earliest forms of hormonal research is to look at the history of castration. Castration may have been man's very first experiment in deliberate—and permanent—endocrine alteration, and its practice since ancient times implies a deep understanding of the link between the male testes and male development and behavior, even if those doing the castration didn't know what testosterone or even a hormone was. Castration was often used as a means of preventing cuckoldry, most famously in Eastern civilizations among harem guards, but it was also used to create reliable administrators—eunuchs were seen as less unruly—and even to produce better male singers. Men castrated before puberty retain a high-pitched singing voice equivalent to a soprano, mezzo-soprano, or contralto, but with a much wider range.

Castration has probably been used as a punishment and torture since man first started turning weapons on himself. There's pretty much no evidence of castration in the ancient archaeological record, though, because it's a soft tissue wound, even when the entire penis (and not just the scrotum) is removed. Unlike, say, cannibalism, which produces distinctive scraping marks on human bones from the removal of flesh, and the breaking of bones to access the marrow, castration leaves no marks on skeletal remains for an archaeologist to interpret.

Castration before puberty does leave some distinct skeletal evidence, though, as scientists are starting to discover. In 2011, scientists exhumed the skeleton of a famous 18th-century *castrato*—an Italian singer castrated before puberty to preserve his angelic voice—and discovered a number of features that could be indicative of pre-pubertal castration.[33] These included unusually long limb bones, incomplete bone fusion, and low limb density (osteoporosis). It was estimated from the only surviving complete limb that this individual was 6'3" tall. The front end of the *castrato*'s skull was also significantly thickened. Similar evidence has since been found in exhumations of other *castrati*.

The first written evidence for castration comes from the Sumerian city of Lagash 4,000 years ago.

China has the longest unbroken tradition of castration, where it became an essential part of bureaucratic and political culture. The earliest records of castration in China date to 1300 BC. Eunuchs were essential to the Chinese administration and even held important political roles. The last Chinese eunuch, Sun Yaoting, died in 1996, aged 94. Castration was performed by licensed surgeons near the imperial court in Beijing. Around 25 percent did not survive the procedure. Eunuchs would keep their severed genitals in a box, which would be buried with them when they died, as depicted in the film *The Last Emperor* (1997). By the end of the Ming dynasty, in the middle of the 17th century, there were maybe 70,000 eunuchs employed in the service of the emperor. Although most were castrated as men, there is some evidence, including skeletal evidence, that some were castrated before puberty.

Eunuchs existed in other ancient civilizations, including Babylonia and Egypt. Castration is central to Greek mythology, and to the myth of the birth of the goddess Aphrodite, as depicted in a famous fresco by the Italian painter Giorgio Vasari (1511–1574). Several million African slaves were castrated in the Islamic empire between about 650 and 1920. They were used for a variety of roles, from labor to soldiering. Self-castration, as a means of extinguishing desire, had an important role to play among certain 'primitive' Christian sects and was seen as a sign of extreme devotion, but later came to be treated by Church authorities as a dangerous sign of radicalism and even heresy, erasing the divinely ordained difference between men and women.

Our ancestors also attempted forms of organotherapy using the testicles, mainly from other animals, which we could consider direct precursors of today's oral, injectable, and gel-based treatments.[34] For example, the Roman natural philosopher Pliny the Elder (23–74) recommended consuming animal testicles to relieve symptoms of fatigue and erectile dysfunction. Similar treatments were prescribed in the Arab world in the 9th century and throughout the Middle Ages. The great philosopher Albert Magnus (1193–1280) prescribed a mixture of powdered hogs' testicles and wine for increased energy and vigor.

Testosterone and Behavior

TODAY WHAT we know scientifically about testosterone's effects on male behavior comes from human and animal studies in a wide variety of different settings, from laboratories to zoos and the jungles of Africa. One common form of human study involves administration of testosterone gel and a placebo to groups of men who are then asked to perform a simple game or perceptual test to see how the hormone affects their behavior and particularly traits like honesty, generosity, and the sense for fair play. From these studies, we're then told that testosterone makes men more honest or that it makes them, say, more willing to tolerate forms of "advantageous inequality."

Here's an example. In a 2023 study in the journal *Psychoneuroendocrinology*, one hundred and twenty young men were either given testosterone gel or a placebo and then asked to play a "dictator game" where they could choose to allocate resources to others exactly as they pleased.[35] According to the researchers, "the testosterone group showed significantly reduced aversion to advantageous inequality. These findings suggest that testosterone facilitates decisions that prioritize selfish economic motives over fairness concerns, which in turn may boost status-enhancing behaviors."

Does testosterone administration make men more comfortable with inequality if it benefits their own status? I'm going to return to this study later because it has important political implications bearing on the difference between right and left, and how testosterone decline might be feeding into current trends in political allegiance. For the time being, note a few things. Note how the findings are coded. The standard frame for these studies—the standard model of thinking, behavior, and values—is implicitly democratic. Any form of thinking or behavior from the research subjects that does not tend towards the maximum benefit for the maximum number of people is automatically defined as anti-social, to be discouraged. Or, to put it in terms that would be comprehensible to the ancient Greeks, we're talking about *thymos*: the *isothymic* versus the *megalothymic*. The desire for equality versus the desire for distinction and self-assertion. The discipline of behavioral psychology is *isothymic* by default, and so are most scientific and academic disciplines. Watch out for that.

These little games can be quite illuminating about particular aspects of testosterone's effects on human behavior. They're useful because you can set them up and monitor them easily within closely defined parameters. But we also need to observe the hormone's effects in more complicated situations, where the possibilities bear more closely on real life.

Animal studies do a lot of the work here. Consider the following animal study, published in August 2022 by researchers at Emory University.[36] "Testosterone promotes 'cuddling,' not just aggression, animal study finds," was the headline in a media release reporting the findings. The research was carried out on Mongolian gerbils and showed that, depending on the context, testosterone could either promote prosocial friendly behavior (cuddling) or aggressive behavior in the face of external threats.

Male gerbils were allowed to bond with female gerbils and get them pregnant. The male gerbils were then given an injection of testosterone. Although the researchers expected that the hormone would make the males less interested in their partners, the opposite happened: the male gerbils became "super partners," spending even more time than normal cuddling with the pregnant females. The males were then separated from their mates and placed in cages with unknown males. Normally, this would result in a serious bust-up between the two males, but again, the opposite happened. This friendly behavior changed immediately, however, when the original males were given another shot of testosterone. Now they chased the intruders or hid away from them. "It was like they suddenly woke up and realized they weren't supposed to be friendly in that context," explained one of the researchers. Testosterone, then, appears to function as a kind of context-specific switch, now favoring nurturing behavior, now favoring aggression, depending on which is appropriate. We're already far from the standard stereotype of testosterone simply as the "aggression hormone."

There are also more complicated human studies, too; although they're fewer and farther between. For example, scientists followed groups of Bolivian hunters and measured levels of testosterone and the so-called "love hormone" oxytocin before, during, and after a hunt.[37] The scientists expected there to be an antagonism between the two hormones, stating that testosterone is associated with status competition—e.g., the hunt itself, where individual skill and distinction generally determine whether a kill happens—but oxytocin is associated with what comes next, such as returning to the village and one's family and sharing the spoils. The scientists noted that studies suggested "parenting and pair-bonding in humans are . . . typically associated with high baseline OT [oxytocin] and low T [testosterone]." It was expected that testosterone and oxytocin would rise and fall independently of each other. Something very different happened, though. Testosterone and oxytocin increased in concert together, and this suggests that testosterone and oxytocin, far from being antagonistic, might be mutually reinforcing. This effect might serve a useful evolutionary purpose, making displays of individual prowess that are socially useful feel pleasurable, as well as other kinds of masculine behavior, including sex and parenting.

The Insidious Effects of Low-T

ANOTHER WAY to understand the complex role of testosterone in masculinity is to look at what happens to men who have low testosterone. What is their life like? How is it different from normal life? We have a wealth of studies associating low testosterone with all sorts of negative health effects, from low libido and erectile dysfunction to anxiety and depression, but the best way to understand what having low testosterone does to a man, to my mind, is to look at personal testimonies from sufferers. Thankfully, the forum website Reddit contains a number of communities dedicated to the problems men suffer as a result of low testosterone.

My favorite subreddit in this regard is r/lowT, which features detailed testimonials from sufferers, corroboration, and advice from fellow sufferers, and also accounts from men who have sorted out their testosterone, usually as a result of testosterone-replacement therapy or TRT (i.e., taking testosterone, whether in pill, injection or gel form).

Here's one short testimony, verbatim.

> So I've dealt with a fairly large amount of depression, fatigue, weight gain, lack of sex drive, etc., for a fairly long time since I was at least 16. I've always been skeptical/worried about some underlying reason to all of this, but every GP I've visited always told me "eat better, exercise, generic healthy lifestyle" as a fix-all for me. I've never had a doctor who would take the initiative to at least do a simple blood test for me.

> This past year, I started visiting a new doctor for regular check-ups and he agreed that I needed a in-depth analysis at [sic] my hormone levels to check for any possible underlying issues I may be having.
>
> After analyzing my blood work, it came to be that I have a testosterone level in the low 300s, and he decided it would be best for me to immediately begin Low-T therapy.[38]

Another user, a twenty-five-year-old man with a low-testosterone diagnosis, describes how he is suicidal, has low self-esteem, has no energy, feels passive and can't make decisions, can't summon any drive to compete and deliberately avoids conflicts, has zero interest in sex, never sleeps well, and has absolutely no ambition or motivation for life in general. These are all classic symptoms associated with having low testosterone, and, as you can imagine, they blight the lives of all men of any age who are unfortunate enough to suffer from them. It's not just impossible for men with low T to do the higher things we associate with being a man; even basic human functions like going to sleep or making decisions are impossible in the worst cases. Men with low testosterone often describe themselves as literal zombies or the walking dead.

Among users of these subreddits who manage to sort out their testosterone, the language is almost uniformly the language of joy, of transformation, and even of rebirth. A pretty typical title for a post might be "Fairly young, hypogonadal [i.e., low testosterone] male, around two weeks into TRT. All I can say is . . . WOW!" or "TRT has changed my life at a young age." For some, the effects are immediate. One user describes how waking up the day after his first testosterone injection "felt like a miracle." "Confidence is coming back and I just feel like my old self." "TRT was the best decision

I've ever made for myself," comments a different user after posting yet another miraculous story.[39]

Millions of men in the U.S. now have low testosterone. That, at least, is uncontroversial. The exact number, though, varies widely depending on who you ask. Worldwide, prevalence of low testosterone in men has been estimated at between 10 and 40 percent—a considerable range.[40] The percentage also varies according to the age of the men in question: older men generally have a significantly higher prevalence of low testosterone. For argument's sake, let's just consider the 10 to 40 percent range. There are roughly 165 million adult men in the U.S. At the lower end of that range, 10 percent, we're talking 16.5 million men, roughly, with low testosterone, and at the upper end, 66 million. That's a vast difference.

A big part of the problem is that there's no universally accepted definition of low testosterone. Hypogonadism, the clinical term for inadequate testosterone production, is defined in terms of serum testosterone level: if your levels are beneath a certain threshold, you're hypogonadal. But one physician will tell you one figure, and another might give you a figure that's half or double that. Some physicians and specialists will say 200 ng/dl of testosterone is the cut-off for low testosterone, while others will say 400 ng/dl. Hypogonadism is defined as being either biochemical—meaning there is biochemical evidence of testosterone deficiency, like damage to the testicles or the inheritance of certain genetic traits—or symptomatic, which means the subject has symptoms consistent with low testosterone (lack of libido, anxiety, low mood, etc.) and also has testosterone levels below the normal range.

Many physicians deal with the significant uncertainly by emphasizing symptomology over laboratory values, and that seems sensible, but it makes quantification for our purposes here more difficult and dependent on men presenting themselves to their physicians for diagnosis and treatment. What's safe to say is that this is already a problem affecting millions of men in the U.S. and around the world, and if the trends continue—and there's no reason to believe they won't—it's a problem that's going to get a lot worse.

Hikikomori Hell

IT'S NOT just Reddit that provides evidence of the devastating spread of testosterone decline among men. We can link it to forms of social withdrawal that are well-documented, especially in Asia. In Japan, there's a widespread social phenomenon known as *hikikomori*. If you've been hanging around the right—or the wrong—places on the internet, you're likely to know about this already. *Hikikomori* refers to the phenomenon itself and the individuals affected by it. Although recluses have existed around the world throughout recorded history—think of hermits or anchorites in the Middle Ages, for example, living in forests and wild places or choosing to be sealed up in cells attached to churches and chapels—the scale of withdrawal from society taking place in Japan is unprecedented. In a country of around 120 million people, widely accepted estimates claim there are at least half a million *hikikomori* under the age of forty, and half a million over that age.[41] The Japanese government reckons there are a further 1.5 million who are also "on the verge" of becoming *hikikomori*.[42] Some believe the phenomenon is far worse than that. A leading Japanese psychiatrist, Saito Tamaki, says there could be as many as ten million *hikikomori* in Japan.[43]

Individuals remain isolated for years or even decades. *Hikikomori* often start out as so-called "school-refusers" or *futoko*, who simply won't go to school. Precise figures on the gender balance of *hikikomori* are difficult to find, but it's widely agreed that the vast majority are men.

Researchers have developed specific diagnostic criteria for the condition as it's grown. [44] These include the following.

+ Spending most of the day and nearly every day confined to home.

+ Marked and persistent avoidance of social situations and social relationships.

+ Social-withdrawal symptoms causing significant functional impairment.

+ A duration exceeding six months.

+ No apparent physical or mental etiology to account for the social withdrawal symptoms.

With studies of the hikikomori phenomenon, there's generally a strong emphasis on the social and cultural factors at work pushing men into isolation—for example, the lack of steady jobs for young people in Japan, the rising average age of the population, and the cultural belief that shame, including shameful people, should be hidden away from society—but it's clear that this phenomenon is, in many ways, continuous with what I've described above in the case of the zombie men of Reddit's r/lowT forum. And by that I mean *hikikomori* is almost certainly a problem of hormones. There's at least one study that shows young Japanese men are more likely to become *hikikomori* if they have low testosterone. [45] The study's abstract lays it out.

Salivary samples were collected from 159 healthy early adolescent boys (mean age [standard deviation]: 11.5 [0.73])
selected from participants of the "population-neuroscience
study of the Tokyo Teen Cohort" . . . Social withdrawal and
confounding factors, such as the secondary sexual characteristics and their age in months, were evaluated by self-ad-
ministered questionnaires completed by the primary parents.
The degree of social withdrawal was assessed with the Child
Behavior Checklist . . . Levels of salivary testosterone, and
cortisol as a control, were measured by liquid chromatog-
raphy-tandem mass spectrometry . . . A higher risk of social
withdrawal was associated with a lower salivary testosterone
level after adjustment for age in months (odds ratio 0.55, 95
percent confidence interval 0.33-0.94), and the association
remained significant after adjusting for body mass index, the
degree of anxiety/depression and pubertal stage.[46]

Emphasis on social and cultural factors isn't enough to
explain why there are also half a million *hikikomori* in
nearby South Korea—it's a different country, after all—or
why "inexplicable numbers of working-age men" some six
or more million, in the U.S. are now going without work
and instead play video games all day, watch porn, and eat
junk food, apparently content with that life, just like their
counterparts in Korea and Japan.[47]

I'm not saying that the problems of millions of young
men in Japan or in the U.S. simply boil down to testosterone, and that millions of doses of TRT would be enough to
solve them in an instant. What I am saying, though, is that
beneath the headline-grabbing problems that are attributed
to social and cultural and economic facts—beneath the
water, so to speak—there lies a much greater biological
problem, one that is largely neglected if it's even mentioned

at all. And the evidence suggests that it's going to get worse: the trends in testosterone levels all point in one direction.

The Men Without (Literal) Chests

"IN A sort of ghastly simplicity we remove the organ and demand the function. We make men without chests and expect of them virtue and enterprise. We laugh at honour and are shocked to find traitors in our midst. We castrate and bid the geldings be fruitful."[48]

When a quotation's that good, it bears repeating.

In his essay, "The Abolition of Man," from which that quotation is taken, C.S. Lewis railed against a particular kind of modern attitude, one which deems all statements of value—"This waterfall is sublime," is his example—as nothing but expressions of the speaker's inner feelings. There are no essences, and nature has the meaning we ascribe to it, and we are therefore free to disagree with it at will, as we choose. Lewis knew, like anybody else intelligent who gives the matter a bit of thought, that consistent moral subjectivism is an impossibility. It's impossible not to value at least some things in a way that suggests we believe they truly are good and worth pursuing in a fundamental, objective sense. But even in Lewis's day, that clear inconsistency didn't prevent subjectivism from becoming a ubiquitous doctrine in education, with dreadful effects.

Lewis knew that the spread of such ideas about morality and the ultimate nature of the world was creating a whole generation of "men without chests." Lewis didn't mean that literally, of course. By "chests" he meant something like "courage." He meant men could no longer behave like men because they couldn't really value what they were meant to value. Right back to the ancient Greeks, the great teachers like Plato, Aristotle, and St. Augustine had taught that the aim of teaching is to make men love what is good and hate what is bad. Without that "chest," man is little better than a beast, possessing none of the means to properly reflect on and act in a truly human manner.

And yet, the metaphors are all biological, physical—organs, chests, castration, geldings.

The truth is, Lewis's argument, like Fukuyama's in the introduction, can be taken that much further, to the biological level. Today, Lewis would be literally right about a generation of men without chests. Men in their millions lack the very physicality required to be fully men, to value what they are meant to value, and to be what they are meant to be—and they lack that physicality because of testosterone decline. The ranks of the men without chests are swelling with each passing day.

Some will still doubt the decline is real. When people want to question the evidence for testosterone decline, they usually say something like, "Testosterone levels vary throughout the day and the studies don't all sample at the same time; therefore they aren't strictly comparable." Or they'll point to the potential effects of sleep deprivation or other transient factors and say that they haven't been controlled for adequately.

Some of this may, no doubt, be true. But what's also true is that male reproductive parameters are collapsing across the board: sperm count, sperm quality, and other hormonal and health markers like cardiovascular health and insulin sensitivity. Sperm counts, in particular, are declining at such a rate that according to one world expert in fertility, within a quarter of a decade, it may actually be impossible for humans to reproduce by natural means. It stands to reason that if other important markers of male health, and testicular health in particular, are collapsing, testosterone is bound to follow.

The best way we can understand testosterone decline is as part of that broader collapse. It's there that we'll find the causes and, perhaps, the solutions too.

CHAPTER 3

Securing the Means of Reproduction

"For the first time in the history of the world, every human being is now subjected to contact with dangerous chemicals, from the moment of conception until death. In the less than two decades of their use, the synthetic pesticides have been so thoroughly distributed throughout the world that they occur virtually everywhere. They have been recovered from most of the major river systems and even from streams of groundwater flowing unseen through the earth. Residues of these chemicals linger in soil to which they have been applied a dozen years before. They have entered and lodged in the bodies of fish, birds, reptiles, and domestic and wild animals so universally that scientists carrying on animal experiments find it almost impossible to locate subjects free from contamination. They have been found in fish in remote mountain lakes, in earthworms burrowing in soil, in the eggs of birds—and in man himself. For these chemicals are now stored in the bodies of the vast majority of human beings, regardless of age. They occur in the mother's milk, and probably in the tissues of the unborn child."

—RACHEL CARSON, *Silent Spring*

— ♦♦♦ —

Testosterone and Fertility Decline

I T's A strangely underappreciated fact today that societies can't reproduce if people don't reproduce. People seem to think societies are always there, transcendental things that will persist regardless of what individual people do. That they're like the sun, the sea, or rocks.

But they're not. Societies have no independent life beyond the people they're made up of. And if the people a society is made up of aren't reproducing, that society isn't reproducing, which means it's in trouble and may, in a worst-case scenario, die. The fact that we, in our modern Western societies, have come to believe there's no need to encourage citizens to reproduce doesn't mean we've somehow broken free of our biological bonds and found a way to make our societies reproduce without people reproducing. Instead, it's simply a function of our unprecedented reliance on immigration to counter population churn. But immigrants must reproduce, too. And, for the most part, they do—usually at much higher rates than the natives of Western countries. But even that's changing, as we'll see.

Virtually every society in history has faced reproductive issues at some point. A society's form largely determines the kind of reproductive issues it will face, although some kinds of reproductive issues are common. While our reproductive issues are similar to those faced by past societies, there are also striking differences that make our situation unique, and perhaps even uniquely grave.

Let's consider some historical examples for a moment. When the means of reproduction were threatened, our ancestors produced a range of responses, some of which we would recognize, while others would seem, frankly, stupid or even deeply immoral.

For the ancient Greeks, fertility was just one aspect of the broader practice of *eugenics*, a word that means something like "coming into being well" or just "good birth." *Eugenics* is a word to conjure with, one of those words you can't say at the dinner table anymore for reasons that scarcely need elaborating. But it's worth reminding ourselves that we make *eugenics* our concern—or maybe a better way to put it would be, eugenics makes *us its concern*, since *eugenics* is rooted in our evolved natures, which have developed and guided our ancestors to this point—whenever we consider a potential mate, even when the aim of mating is not child-bearing but momentary pleasure.

Analysis of user behavior on dating apps reveals striking regularities in preferences for mate selection, as well the extent to which those apps are changing our behavior. Any masculinity guru worth his salt will tell you that Tinder has unleashed a phenomenon known as "hypergamy," in which a small minority of attractive, eligible men get all the women and have all the sex, and the rest of the men don't even get scraps. A slightly more sophisticated thinker like Jordan B. Peterson would say something like, "Women mate up dominance hierarchies and men mate across and down dominance hierarchies," but it amounts to the same thing.

For a long time, I've had the idea to compare the bleak landscape of dating apps to the detailed *eugenic* scheme laid out in Plato's *Republic,* a book we'll return to. There are interesting parallels between the elaborate social arrangements Plato describes to ensure *eugenic* matches between the elite citizens of the ideal republic and the way hypergamy on dating apps filters the sexes. The main difference, of course, is that the *eugenic* scheme of Plato's ideal republic leads to childbirth, whereas the republic of Tinder simply leads to sex. Hypergamy also creates enormous resentment among unsuccessful men, something Plato was very careful to avoid by ensuring that all male citizens would get to have sex. Plato, at least, knew that a horde of angry, unfuckable men would be a serious destabilizing agent for any society.

Ancient Greek Fertility Hacks

BUT WHAT do *eugenic* practices in ancient Greece tell us about the kind of fertility problems the ancient Greeks encountered? In most Greek cities, "mere" fertility was not usually the main *eugenic* consideration, but a subsidiary of others. This is reflected, as I've noted, in Plato's insistence that the elite should be encouraged to reproduce only with each other, and not to dilute their gene pool by mating with the lower classes. Being able to produce enough people for society to continue—full stop—wasn't generally in question.

In ancient Sparta, however, it was. *Oligandria,* "the scarcity of men," was recognized as a constant threat to the continuation of Sparta's military society. Spartan responses to *oligandria,* including the worship of specific gods linked to fertility and the cultivation of links with Alexandria (the center of medicine in the known world) are examined in a fascinating short paper in the journal *Hormones.*[49]

> One of the most critical problems that classical Sparta faced was oligandria, the decline in the number of Spartan male citizens who had civil rights and were capable of fighting for Sparta. Recurrent wars, either conquering or defensive, unremitting and grueling military drilling, battle wounds and numerous war fatalities caused the population of Sparta's common male citizens—this did not include the population of helots and perioikoi—to chronically be in decline. [50]

According to Aristotle, in his *Politics*, *oligandria* was one of the reasons why women in Sparta had more power than elsewhere in ancient Greece: their role in producing vital male warriors. Aristotle went so far as to attribute Sparta's decline from its maximum to the excessive power of Spartan women. He called Sparta a *gynecocracy*—a "hen-pecked society."

What did the Spartans do to try and raise the birth rate and keep the warriors rolling off the production line? The paper in *Hormones* tells us they devoted considerable resources to the worship of goddesses of fertility, like Helen, Orthia Artemis, Artemis Cyparissia and Artemis Eilithia, and that they developed new fertility-boosting potions through the expansion of medicine as a discipline, in contact with experts in Alexandria. We know the Spartans used concoctions of *agnus castus*, for example, to treat infertility in women. Scientific studies have shown this plant does indeed have beneficial hormonal effects for women: it can help regulate periods, reduce premenstrual tension, and ease the transition to menopause. Another thing the Spartans did on the male side was introduce a system where older men who were impotent or otherwise unable to attend to their wives sexually would select and invite younger men to consort with them and produce offspring.

Nomads and Gonads

LET'S LOOK at another very different warrior society, again from the ancient Greek world. The Scythians faced fertility problems too, and, like the problems faced by the Spartans, they were largely determined by the nature of their lifestyle. These horse-riding Indo-Iranian nomads lived on the Caspian-Pontic steppe in modern-day Russia and Ukraine and were a fixture of ethnographic descriptions like those of Herodotus in the *Histories*. Scythian mercenaries in Greek cities often functioned as a kind of police force. They were the butt of constant jokes by playwrights like Aristophanes. Nomadic societies are often thought of as being the pinnacle of virility and contrasted favorably with neighboring agricultural societies, whose peoples are described as less healthy and less bellicose, but this isn't entirely true.

Scythian fertility problems were described at length in a medical text called *On Airs, Water and Places*, by a Greek writer known as "Pseudo-Hippocrates," who wrote in the 5th century BC.[51] According to Pseudo-Hippocrates, the cold, damp environment of the Caspian-Pontic steppe affected the Scythians' bodies, and especially their humors, making them "soft and moist." Remember that this was the age of the Four Humors when it was believed the body was made up of four substances (blood, black bile, yellow bile, and phlegm) that must be kept in balance to avoid ill health. This imbalance in the Scythians' humors was made worse by their lifestyle, which involved long periods in the saddle or—for the women—in the famous Scythian wagons rolling along behind the horses.

Pseudo-Hippocrates noted that the women became quite overweight because they spent so much time sitting in their wagons. "The girls get amazingly flabby and pudgy," he said. Just how flabby and pudgy is unclear. It's likely that

Scythian women wouldn't have been fat enough to star in a modern underwear advert, but by ancient standards, at least, their weight was unusual, and therefore worthy of comment. Pseudo-Hippocrates adds that "People of such a constitution [meaning both sexes] cannot be prolific"—i.e., reproduce in large number—a fact he attributes to the women's extra weight and, interestingly, to the effects of the Scythians' hard saddles on the male reproductive organs.

Even more interesting is the description Pseudo-Hippocrates provides of an entire class of sterile men who embraced the fact that they were, for all intents and purposes, women, and chose to behave as such. Yes, there were transgenders on the Caspian-Pontic steppe in the Bronze Age. These people were treated with a kind of divine wonder:

> There are many eunuchs among the Scythians who perform female work and speak like women . . . such persons are called *andrieis* ("effeminates"). The Scythians attribute the cause of their impotence to god, and venerate and worship such persons, everyone dreading that a similar fate might befall himself.[52]

The Scythians saw being struck with effeminacy as an act of God, but Pseudo-Hippocrates believed it was caused, again, by horse-riding. According to his observations, there were more eunuchs among the higher classes because they spent more time in the saddle than the lower classes, who generally lived like agriculturalists, tending the land, rather than freewheeling nomads. "[The rich men] always wear trousers and spend most of their time on horseback, unable to fondle themselves, and from cold and fatigue they forget their sexual desires."

To some extent, Pseudo-Hippocrates must have been playing up Greek stereotypes about barbarians and the superiority of Greek culture. Ethnocentrism, with its "us and them" tendency, is as old and as inescapable as humanity itself. Archaeological evidence reveals the Scythians to have been unusually tall and robust, or at least those who were high status enough to receive elaborate *kurgan* ("barrow") burials full of grave goods, including weaponry, horses, livestock, and some of the most beautiful gold artifacts ever discovered in the ancient world. There is also evidence that some Scythian women really did fight alongside men in battle, as Herodotus tells us they did, which would have required physical capabilities and fitness well beyond those of the average body-positivity influencer today.[53] Even so, the lifestyle factors Pseudo-Hippocrates describes—especially weight gain, long periods of sitting, tight trousers, and constant pressure on the male genitalia from saddles—would all have had detrimental effects on fertility.

Obese Women and Tight Trousers

OBESITY IS clearly linked to testosterone decline: the heavier you are, the lower your testosterone is likely to be. Studies show that overweight men have lower sperm quality and quantity too.[54] Women who are overweight have difficulty conceiving and an increased rate of miscarriage.[55] Sitting for long periods is associated with reduced fertility in men for two reasons: first, because it is associated with being overweight, and second because it impedes proper thermoregulation of the testes.[56] The testes overheat. Tight underwear and tight trousers have both been shown to reduce men's reproductive health.[57] Again, this is probably because tight underwear and trousers affect thermoregulation. In the case of tight underwear, it may also be because of polyester's ability to induce a static-electric charge across the testes, which disrupts the structure and function of testicular cells. Wearing a polyester "sling"—e.g., a tight pair of polyester underwear—for a period of months has been shown to be a 100 percent effective, and apparently reversible, form of male contraception.[58] (If you and your wife or girlfriend are looking to conceive, one of the first things you should do, gentlemen, is get some loose all-cotton boxers and stop wearing tight jeans.) And as far as hard saddles are concerned, it's well documented that keen male cyclists regularly suffer infertility.[59] Disrupted thermoregulation and physical damage to the testes are likely to be the main causes, although hormonal changes, chronic stress, and the production of large quantities of reactive oxygen species—particles that cause damage to natural tissues—may also be to blame.

If the Scythians really did labor with serious fertility problems, we don't know what they did in response, apart from attempting to propitiate the gods and avoid being turned into *andrieis* themselves, as Pseudo-Hippocrates tells us. They may, like the Spartans, have resorted to medical concoctions. Their reaction may have been like that of the Comanche of the American Plains, another horsebound warrior society that struggled to reproduce. Commentators of the 19th century and later historians noted that Comanche women miscarried at extremely high rates because they were forced to ride long distances even while pregnant. Unlike the Scythians, the Comanche did not have wooden wagons for their women to rest in as they traveled.

The Comanche Solution

INSTEAD OF worshipping fertility goddesses or cultivating medicinal remedies, the Comanche attempted to secure the means of reproduction violently by intensifying their raids on European frontier settlements and other Native American tribes. Comanche raiders would kill all the men, male children, and old women they found and then strap the remaining young girls and women to their saddles and take them back to Comancheria. Among the more famous captives was nine-year-old Cynthia Parker. In 1836, she was kidnapped during a Comanche raid in North Texas. Her fate was to become the bride of a powerful Comanche chief and give birth to Quanah Parker, the last and greatest of all the Comanche chiefs. (S.C. Gwynne's book on Quanah, *Empire of the Summer Moon*,[60] is very much worth your time.)

So what does any of this have to do with us today? Every society probably faces reproductive problems at one time or another, and those reproductive problems and any response to them bear the distinct imprint of that society and its way of life. We are no different. In fact, our problems have taken on the proportions of a crisis unlike any faced by a human society before. The reproductive problems we face have the potential to destroy us, and soon.

The Decline Scales Up

TODAY'S TESTOSTERONE decline is part of a broader decline in fertility, and must be treated as such, within its context, if we are to understand it properly and at least try to do something about it. This stands to reason. We wouldn't expect one of the principal indexes of maleness to decline so stunningly in isolation. If men's testes are no longer producing testosterone in the way they were or should be, then that probably means they're not producing the other things they were or should be—and that means, principally, sperm. We have a wealth of evidence to suggest that however bad the decline in testosterone may be in recent decades, the decline

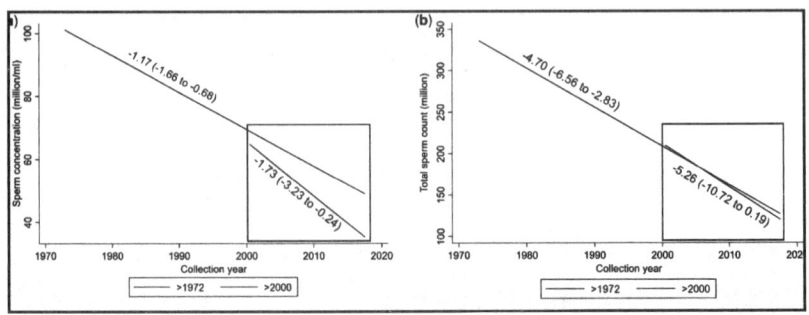

META-REGRESSION MODELS FOR MEAN SPERM CONCENTRATION (SC) AND TOTAL SPERM COUNT (TSC) BY COLLECTION YEAR AMONG UNSELECTED MEN FROM ALL CONTINENTS, HUMAN REPRODUCTION UPDATE, 2022[61]

in sperm—in both their quantity and their quality—is even worse.

In fact, within a matter of decades, the decline may be so bad that we could face a "spermageddon" situation, in which men produce so few sperm that mankind might have trouble reproducing by natural means at all.

If current trends continue, by 2050 the median sperm count will be zero, which means that one-half of all men will produce no sperm at all, and the other half will produce so few that they might as well produce none, because they certainly won't be getting a woman pregnant, no matter how hard they try.

What's distinctive about our current reproductive decline, what makes it different from those of Sparta or ancient Scythia, is not just the scale and gravity of the problem. It's also the central role of man-made chemicals and, in particular, a class of chemicals known as "endocrine disruptors" for their damaging effects on our hormonal (i.e., endocrine) system. Humans have never been exposed to endocrine-disrupting chemicals in the way that we are today, for the simple fact that they didn't exist until the industrial age. Sure, there are natural endocrine disruptors—soy and hops being good examples—but exposure to these substances was trivial in the pre-industrial age. Today, our environment is, quite literally, saturated with endocrine disruptors—the food, the water, the air—and we can expect to come into contact with them from the moment we are conceived, in the apparent safety of the womb, until the day we die. There's no escape.

The possibility of an approaching spermageddon received significant attention in 2021 when Professor Shanna Swan, one of the world's leading reproductive health experts, published *Count Down: How Our Modern World Is Threatening Sperm Counts, Altering Male and Female Reproductive Development, and Imperiling the Future of the Human Race*.[62] Professor Swan appeared on all the major podcasts, including the Joe Rogan Experience, and for a time it was almost impossible to avoid discussions of falling sperm rates and testosterone, and how babies' ano-genital distance— the distance between the genitals and anus—is shrinking because of exposure to harmful chemicals like PFAS and phthalates before birth.

A Looming Spermageddon

RUMBLINGS OF spermageddon have been audible for decades. Swan herself was drawn to the topic of male fertility decline by a study published in the *British Medical Journal* in 1992,[63] often referred to as "the Carlsen paper," that claimed a significant reduction in sperm counts in the last fifty years. Like many others at the time, Professor Swan was skeptical of the findings, believing the methodology was probably flawed, and that the findings were therefore wrong and alarmist. When she was appointed in 1994 to the National Academy of Sciences Committee on Hormonally Active Agents in the Environment, she was asked by the Committee if the conclusions in the Carlsen paper were true. Together with two other researchers, Swan went over the paper with a fine-tooth comb:

> The results were utterly astounding: after six months of data crunching and considering potential biases and confounding factors, our overall conclusion agreed, almost exactly, with that of the Carlsen team. Because we'd accounted for geographic location in the various studies, we'd found that sperm counts really *were* declining in the United States and Europe.[64]

Swan's findings were published in 1997, and she then spent the next twenty years researching fertility, publishing dozens and dozens of articles on the subject. In 2017, she published a landmark meta-analysis—a study of studies—of nearly 200 papers on sperm counts over a period of 50 years that confirmed beyond a shadow of a doubt the full extent of the recent decline in male fertility parameters:

> Between 1973 and 2011, sperm concentrations (the number of sperm per millilitre of semen) dropped more than 52 percent among random men in Western countries; meanwhile the total sperm count fell by more than 59 percent. We came to these conclusions after examining the findings from 185 studies involving 42,935 men that had been conducted during this thirty-eight-year period. To be clear: these men weren't selected based on their fertility status; they were everyday Joes and Johns, ordinary men.[65]

So sperm counts among normal Western men halved in a period of just forty years.

The meta-analysis was enormously influential, becoming the 26th-most cited scientific paper of that year and spawning an alarmed response in the mainstream media, just like Professor Swan's book *Count Down* would a few years later: "Going, Going, Gone? Human Sperm Counts Are Plunging" (*Psychology Today*)[66]; "Sperm Count Drop Could Make Humans Extinct" (BBC)[67]; "Who's Killing America's Sperm?" (*Newsweek*).[68]

Professor Swan explicitly links male fertility decline to testosterone decline. She describes low testosterone as a "hidden player in the men's infertility picture." "This makes sense," she says, "since adequate testosterone is needed to produce healthy sperm, and many of the factors that can lower sperm count can effect male hormone levels." Testosterone decline and fertility decline are "parallel manifestations of a common source of disruption."[69]

So what is the "common source of disruption," according to Professor Swan? First of all, it would be better to say "sources," since there's clearly no single cause at work. In *Count Down*, Professor Swan goes into great detail discussing how obesity, sedentary lifestyles, smoking, sexually transmitted diseases, and other factors I've talked about have a serious negative effect on fertility for both sexes, not just men. I'll return to women's fertility later. Our fertility crisis is multi-factorial, as they say, and in this sense it isn't different from the problems faced by the ancient Greeks or the Scythians.

Silent, Ubiquitous Threats

BUT ONE factor stands out for its novelty: our exposure to harmful industrial and agricultural chemicals, and, in particular, to endocrine disruptors. Swan describes endocrine disruptors as "silent, ubiquitous threats," and she makes them one of the principal focuses of her book, not least because most people don't know a thing about them.

When I get into the Alex Jones "gay frogs conspiracy theory"—the claim that chemicals in the food and water, put there deliberately, are feminizing men and even causing them to become transgender—I'll discuss why our food supply and environment have become so poisoned by these chemicals, and why we seem to do so little about this, despite the overwhelming body of evidence for the negative health effects. I'll also consider the strongest possible claim about the effects of persistent exposure to endocrine disruptors: that they cause gender dysphoria and transgenderism. The *prima facie* case for this, once you understand the basic facts about human sexual development and the effects of endocrine disruptors, has always been strong, and the ridicule Alex Jones received for his famous "gay frogs" rant was totally undeserved. And not only that: at a stroke the relationship between endocrine disruptors and transgenderism was made a polarizing "culture war" issue when it really shouldn't be. This prevented serious investigation of this issue for a decade, even as rates of gender dysphoria and transgenderism have exploded. Thankfully, there's new research that should see the "conspiracy theory" label torn up, thrown in the bin, and set on fire. Alex Jones was *right*, ladies and gentlemen.

Here, in this chapter, I want to consider what endocrine disruptors are, how they produce their effects, and what some of the main types are.

Endocrine disruptors are chemicals that can interfere with the body's hormonal, or endocrine, system. Because hormones govern pretty much every single process in the human body in some way, that means endocrine disruptors can have effects on just about every single part and function of the body. They can cause fertility problems ranging from malformed genitals and reduced sperm counts to conditions like endometriosis and polycystic ovarian syndrome, but they can also cause early puberty, altered immune function, cancers, diabetes, obesity, respiratory problems, and neurological disabilities. This generality is worth remembering: If there's a synthetic chemical that can mimic the behavior of a natural hormone, exposure to it can disrupt the natural processes associated with that hormone in the body.

Xenoestrogens

ONE OF the most common hormones that's mimicked by endocrine disruptors—by everything from chemicals that make plastics more bendy to herbicides and food additives—is estrogen. Researchers say that such chemicals are "estrogenic" or that they are "xenoestrogens," meaning "estrogens from outside [the body]." We've already seen that the body's testosterone-to-estrogen ratio is crucial for determining proper sexual development. If you're a man, you need much more testosterone than estrogen, and if you're a woman, you need the opposite: more estrogen, much less testosterone. Note, however, that the actual ratios are important. Men don't want infinite testosterone and the smallest possible amount of estrogen, and women don't want infinite estrogen and the smallest possible amount of testosterone. The ratios have to be right. This is why exposure to estrogenic chemicals that upset our proper ratios of sex hormones is a danger to women as well as men, even if estrogen is the "female" hormone.

Ensuring the correct ratios of sex hormones in the body is critical during pregnancy. Professor Swan calls pregnancy, especially the first trimester (the first twelve weeks), a "window of vulnerability," when exposure to endocrine disruptors can disrupt sexual development, with lifelong irreversible effects. The early "reproductive programming window," as it's called, sees the growth and development of the sexual organs. Although biological sex is determined at the moment of conception, depending on the sex chromosomes present (XX for girls and XY for boys), in the early days of the first trimester the genital tract remains undifferentiated. At eight weeks, changes begin to occur that will set in place the proper formation of the genitals according to sex. In boys, that means the development of the penis and testes and the population of germ cells within the testes, which will go on during adolescence to mature into sperm. A process called "minipuberty" then takes place, as a surge of testosterone and other androgens flow in between two and four months after conception, and this process is also highly sensitive to influence by endocrine disruptors.

Maybe the best way to think about this process is to see it as a move away from being female, as Professor Swan explains:

> Looked at another way, female is the default sex for human beings; it's the body's go-to biological sex unless certain hormones swing into action to masculinize the reproductive organs and brain. To become male, the previously uncommitted genitals need to develop into testicles, the scrotum, the penis, and other organs; meanwhile, the testicles need to produce enough testosterone at the right time to complete the journey to physical masculinity. The amount of testosterone that's present in a male fetus after the second month of masculinity is a major factor in determining the size of his penis and other parts of his genitals at birth. By the twenty-second week of pregnancy, the testicles have formed in the abdomen and already contain immature sperm; before long, they'll begin their gradual

descent to the scrotum, reaching their ultimate destination late in pregnancy and, in some boys, even after birth.[70]

In the next chapter, we'll look at the havoc caused by prenatal exposure to one vicious estrogenic chemical in particular. In the mid-20th century, Diethylstilbestrol (DES) was given to millions of pregnant women with a history of miscarriage in an effort to prevent further difficulties bringing a baby to term. Exposure to DES in utero has been linked to terrible reproductive abnormalities in both sexes, including undescended testicles and micropenises in boys, and ectopic pregnancies, miscarriages, premature births and cancers including vaginal and breast cancer. And now, with a recent French study, exposure to DES in utero has also been linked to a vastly increased probability of gender dysphoria and transgenderism in men.

Endocrine Disruptors in History

THE PERMANENT effects caused by prenatal exposure to endocrine disruptors are often referred to as "organizational effects" to distinguish them from the potentially more transitory, or "activational," effects of exposure during adulthood—although the difference between the two quickly becomes blurred when we realize that even small, brief exposures to endocrine-disrupting chemicals in the womb can induce permanent changes to brain structures in ways that might make the child behave in a way that is less typical of its gender after birth. We'll consider this in the next chapter, too.

We've been aware of the estrogenic effects of certain chemicals for decades, but the term "endocrine disruptor" and genuine worry about the effects of exposure to these particular chemicals is much more recent. The first use of "endocrine disruptor" appears to date to a conference held in 1991, and one of the earliest uses in the scientific literature was in a paper published in the journal *Environmental Health Perspectives* two years later.[71] In 2013, the World Health Organisation and the United Nations released a detailed report on endocrine disruptors that called for more research into their effects.[72] The report lays out a comprehensive program to improve our knowledge of endocrine disruptors, beginning with new testing methods to identify endocrine disruptors and including better reporting standards for chemical products—so scientists and the general public can understand what's actually in them—and the sharing of data between scientists and between countries.

The claim that, through modern industrial and agricultural processes, we might be creating a toxic environment on a scale never before seen, with unknown but potentially devastating effects for humans and other life, was mooted as early as the 1960s, most famously in Rachel Carson's 1962 book *Silent Spring*.[73] Carson focused particularly on the massive use of the pesticide DDT, documenting the harms it caused to soldiers during World War II and claiming that the chemical industry was involved in a systematic campaign of disinformation about the chemical's effects, which scientists and government were only too ready to believe. The book received furious pushback from chemical manufacturers, of course, but the public, and eventually government, listened. DDT was banned for agricultural purposes in the U.S., and less than a decade later, the U.S. Environmental Protection Agency was created by President Richard Nixon.

Despite high-profile bans on chemicals like DDT and the creation of regulatory organizations like the EPA, the situation hasn't got much better. In fact, it's probably become far worse. There are even more synthetic chemicals—so many we can only estimate their numbers—they're even more ubiquitous, and we don't have a clue what the vast majority of them even do when they come into contact with human and animal life. Those we do test, we test in ways that fail to take into account their full potential to do harm. Here's Professor Swan again.

> Even decades after the 1976 Toxic Substances Act was enacted, few of the approximately eight-five thousand chemicals that have been produced for use in commercial products, many of which have been identified as potential threats to human health, have even been tested, let alone banned or regulated. In the rare instances when chemicals *are* tested, the studies that are conducted don't usually protect human health because the protocols don't address the effects of dosing nuances (high versus low, for example). Or, they don't consider the potentially cumulative or interactive effects these substances can have when they're mixed inside the human body.[74]

Attempts to regulate persistent organic pollutants, otherwise known as "POPs," have largely amounted to nothing. These chemicals, which linger in the environment and in living creatures for years, decades, or even longer, include DDT, dioxins, and hexachlorobenzene. A schedule of twelve POPs listed for elimination was issued by the 2004 Stockholm Convention on Persistent Organic Pollutants, but the U.S. hasn't even ratified the treaty and, in any case, because of their chemical stability these harmful substances will remain in the environment—in the food, water, air, and soil—long after any ban on their use.

Non-persistent chemicals, by contrast, have much shorter lifespans. Whereas a chemical like DDT has a half-life of fifteen years—meaning it takes fifteen years for concentrations of the chemical to reduce by half in the natural environment—chemicals like phthalates and bisphenol A have half-lives of hours or days. They're gone from the environment and our bodies in a short period of time. The problem with these non-persistent chemicals is that we are constantly being exposed to them, especially through plastics and consumer products, so levels in our bodies are regularly being topped off or added to.

The Most Common Threats

SOME OF the most common non-persistent chemicals include a class of chemicals called phthalates. They're used in everything from plastic products, vinyl floor and wall coverings, and medical devices, to personal-care products like perfumes, hair sprays, soaps, and shampoos. Phthalates are detectable in urine, blood, and breast milk. Three of the worst phthalates identified by Professor Swan are di-2-ethylhexyl-phthalate (DEHP), dibutyl phthalate (DBP) and butyl benzyl phthalate (BBzP), all of which can reduce the body's natural production of testosterone.

> Of these three notorious phthalates, DEHP appears to be the most damaging to the male reproductive system. A 2018 review of research on the subject found "robust evidence of an association between DEHP and DBP exposure and male reproductive outcomes," including shorter AGD [ano-genital distance], reduced semen quality, and lower testosterone levels with DEHP, and reduced semen quality and a longer time to achieving pregnancy with DBP. Men with higher exposure to phthalates also tend to have lower sperm counts and more abnormally shaped sperm.[75]

These three chemicals are scheduled to be phased out in Europe soon, but their use in the U.S. shows no signs of being brought to an end.

Pthalates are also known to affect the developing brain in serious ways. A 2023 study showed that children exposed to phthalates in utero, and in particular, DEHP, have smaller brains and lower IQs when they reach adolescence.[76]

Another non-persistent chemical of great concern is bisphenol A, commonly known as BPA. BPA was first synthesized at the end of the 19th century, and its estrogenic qualities were identified in the 1930s by British scientist Edward Charles Dodds, who was searching for artificial compounds to mimic estrogen. Dodds eventually chose DES for his experiments instead of BPA. By the 1950s, BPA started being used in resins and early plastics, protective coatings, piping, and the lining of food cans. In the intervening decades, it's been added to such a wide variety of products—even to the thermal paper that's used in receipts—that we can truly claim that BPA is a ubiquitous chemical, despite its estrogenicity. Professor Swan notes, for example, that Chinese factory workers with detectable levels of BPA in their urine "were more than four times as likely to have lower sperm counts, more than three times as likely to have poorer sperm vitality, and more than twice as likely to have lower sperm motility than those with undetectable BPA in their urine."[77]

BPA has received a lot of public attention in recent years, especially for its use in products like sippy cups for babies and water bottles for people of all ages, and this has led to the emergence of replacement chemicals and new products that are proudly labeled "BPA-free." Start typing "BPA-free" in the Amazon search bar and a whole range of products will pop up. The problem with these products and the new chemicals that they contain is that they're often just as bad as, if not worse than, bisphenol A. Take bisphenol S (BPS), for example, which has also been shown by multiple studies to be viciously estrogenic.[78] BPS has also been shown to have worrying metabolic effects in mice, causing their brown fat tissue—"metabolically expensive" fat that is involved in regulation of body temperature—to be converted to white fat tissue, which has lower caloric demands. What this means, in effect, is that exposure to BPS can make mice put on weight and become obese without eating more, simply by reducing their bodies' caloric needs.[79] Many endocrine-disrupting chemicals, from BPA and BPS to pesticides like chlorpyrifos, have these obesogenic effects. Weight gain is a serious risk factor for reduced testosterone and fertility, as we've seen, which makes the attack these chemicals wage on our bodies that much more insidious.

I could carry on listing different chemicals and their well-attested endocrine-disrupting effects—per- and polyfluoroalkyl substances (PFAS), polybrominated biphenyls, polybrominated diphenyl ethers, glyphosate, atrazine, and other herbicides—but by now you get the idea. What's even more concerning is an emerging problem that combines the worst aspects of these endocrine disruptors with new threats not just to our fertility but to every aspect of our health, from our breathing and digestion to our minds and our sight.

The Microplastic Menace

IF YOU'VE followed my work on Twitter or read my essays, you'll know that I write about microplastics—tiny pieces of plastic, often imperceptible to the naked eye—a lot. I've described them as "the invisible enemy" and "the microplastic menace," and I carp on about them as much as I do because I think they're that important. I want you to know about them, and I also want you to protect yourself against them, to the extent that you can. I'm not the only one talking about this, either. Professor Swan discusses microplastics at length in *Count Down*, and a wide range of scientists, health experts, and organizations are warning that further research is urgently needed to understand their full arsenal of effects before we cause an irreversible calamity, although some believe we have already reached that point. Certainly, if microplastics are driving the human reproductive crisis and helping push men towards "spermageddon," then I think it's safe to say we've reached the point of catastrophe already.

The term "microplastics" was first introduced in 2004 by Professor Richard Thompson, a marine biologist based in the UK, but it's only in the last five or so years that alarm about microplastics, fueled by media coverage, has really grown.[80]

Microplastics are vehicles or vectors for harmful endocrine-disrupting chemicals, carrying them deep into our bodies and also polluting the environment with them to an extent that makes avoiding them more or less impossible. Because microplastics are made of plastic, they contain harmful plastic chemicals already, but they can also acquire other chemicals in the environment, including persistent organic pollutants, and transfer them into living organisms. The plastic pieces themselves aren't just carriers, though. They have physical effects all of their own, which include hormonal effects. It's been shown, for example, that microplastics are absorbent and can literally "suck up" hormones and other important substances in the blood, including testosterone, making these unavailable to the body for use.[81]

Scientists have discovered that microplastics are everywhere. And when I say "everywhere," I really mean *everywhere*. Microplastics have been found in large quantities in places humans have never set foot, in the most remote locations, and they've also been detected in virtually every single human and animal tissue. Microplastics have been found in lung and gut tissue, in the blood, in the liver and kidneys, in the heart, in the placenta and amniotic fluid that cushions babies in the womb, and even in the eyes, testicles, and penis—the actual "meat" of the penis, I mean. A study published last year found microplastics in every semen sample tested.[82]

Microplastics have become a force of nature, drifting in the air and falling in rain and snow over human settlements and vast tracts of wilderness, and they also accumulate and circulate in our homes in dust, which we inhale. Our homes and our diet are probably our greatest single source of exposure to microplastics today. And the problem is only growing, because our reliance on plastic is growing.

More than nine billion tons of plastics are estimated to have been produced between 1950 and 2017, and more than half of that total was produced since 2004. The vast majority of plastic ends up not in the bin or a landfill or recycling center, but out there, in the environment. Once in the environment, it breaks down through weathering, exposure to UV light from the sun, and digestion by organisms of all kinds into smaller and smaller pieces. Below a certain size, about 5mm, plastics become microplastics, and then below 1,000 nanometres—about 1/100th the width of a human hair—they become nanoplastics. I'm going to use "microplastics" to refer to both microplastics and nanoplastics interchangeably unless I'm referring specifically to one or the other, in which case I'll make it clear.

Microplastics that start off big and end up small are called "secondary" microplastics. But there's also a whole class of "primary" microplastics, classified as such because they're intended to be very small in the first place. These include things like so-called "microbeads" that are used in exfoliating cosmetic products, and they also break down into even smaller pieces, becoming secondary microplastics.

The Scale of the Microplastic Problem

LET'S LOOK at two studies that illustrate nicely the depth and scale of the microplastic problem. The first study made the news a few years ago.[83] Scientists revealed that thousands of tons of microplastics are deposited over Switzerland each year in snow. The researchers collected samples of snow from the tip of the Hoher Sonnenblick mountain in Austria and then used mass spectrometry to identify precise quantities of microplastics in them. According to the scientists' calculations, 43 trillion pieces of microplastic land across Switzerland each year, the equivalent of 3,000 tons. Using meteorological data, the researchers also showed that while a significant proportion of the microplastics (around 30 percent) came from mostly urban areas within a radius of 130 miles from Hoher Sonnenblick, as much as 10 percent may have come from winds and weather taking place in the Atlantic, 1,200 miles away.

There are two important takeaways from this study. First, nowhere on earth, however remote, is untouched by plastic pollution. As we learned in another study published a year later, not even the Antarctic escapes.[84] Second, microplastics circulate as a kind of "force of nature," as part of natural systems—wind, rain and snow, river and sea currents—on the grandest scale, across massive distances.

We're also starting to discover that animals, from birds and fish to insects like bees, ants, and even mosquitoes, are living vehicles for microplastics to be moved on varying scales, too. A 2024 study, for example, showed that mosquitoes ingest microplastics as larvae from the watery environments into which they hatch, and can then transmit them into the skin and blood of animals they feed on, including humans.[85]

And you thought mosquitoes couldn't get any more annoying. Well, they can.

The second of our two studies is more recent. Last year, Chinese scientists demonstrated that microplastics are found in significant quantities inside people's *eyeballs*, in the vitreous humor, the mass of liquid that sits behind the lens.[86] Samples were taken from the eyeballs of forty-nine people suffering from a range of different eye conditions and subjected to a set of complicated analytical techniques. The results showed that there were nearly 1,800 plastic pieces, most of a size of about 50 μm (1/20th of a millimeter) or less, in those forty-nine samples. That works out at about thirty-five fibers per sample on average. The real quantity in each eyeball would be much more.

The researchers noted that there was a close relationship between the number of fibers in each sample and the severity of visual problems experienced by the patient it was taken from. Basically, the more microplastics in your eyes, the more likely you'll have visual problems. Makes sense.

The real question raised by this study is: How did the plastic get there in the first place?

Internally, via the blood, is the most obvious route. The eye has an enormous network of vessels running over its surface and through it. We know that microplastics get into the blood, from the gut and lungs mainly, and from there reach all the major organs of the body. Studies have found microplastics in human brain, heart, lung, liver, womb, and genital tissue. Animal studies have shown microplastics crossing the blood-brain barrier, the brain's only line of defense against pathogens and harmful substances. Polystyrene microplastics fed to mice ended up in their brains within just two hours.[87]

Microplastics could also enter the eye from its outer surface, first by coming into contact with the front of the eye and then, through blinking, migrating to the sides and back of the eye, where there are large numbers of exposed blood vessels. Microplastics in dust land on the eye, but contact lenses could also transfer significant quantities of microplastics onto the surface of the eye. A pair of reusable contact lenses has been estimated to shed over 90,000 plastic particles in a year of wear.[88]

An even more disconcerting possibility: microplastics are in our eyes from birth. A recent study shows that when pregnant mice are fed polystyrene microplastics in water at "environmentally realistic concentrations," the microplastics end up in the eyes of their offspring, where they interfere with the proper development and function of the organ.[89] Microplastics cross the placental barrier from mother to baby in humans, and they've also been found in the amniotic fluid in which babies float for the duration of their term.

The scale of the problem is undeniable. Endocrine disruptors are everywhere. They're simply inescapable. And their effects on fertility and reproductive health, even if you have doubts about the impending approach of spermageddon, are also undeniable. We're talking about thousands upon thousands of scientific studies.

Any attempt to address, let alone solve, the problem of exposure to these chemicals will require massive organization at a national and international level. At present, this isn't happening, and there's very little suggestion that it will occur any time soon. I often joke that if these chemicals had different effects—say, if they increased testosterone instead of decreasing it, and made men more assertive and confident instead of sapping them of their vitality—then governments would already have banned them all by now and scrubbed the environment clean. As facetious as this might sound. I think there's something to it. We really should be asking ourselves why, as evidence mounts, governments seem so untroubled by the threat posed to our health and our ability to fulfil our central biological purpose, to reproduce.

Docile Males and Replacement Migration

PUT TO one side the behavioral effects of exposure to these chemicals, the fact that they make the population, especially males, more docile and easier to control. Part of the reason why Western governments are so untroubled by the endocrine disruptors, I suspect, is because they have a massive standing reserve of reproducers in the non-Western world just waiting to come here. It's no secret that Western nations are importing these positive birth rates. Without constant massive infusions from abroad, Western nations would struggle to maintain a net balance of babies.

Replacement migration, as it's called, is not a conspiracy theory. It's real, and it's central to the planning of Western governments, from Germany to Canada. In July of 2023, for example, German Chancellor Olaf Scholz admitted that his country needs 1.5 million immigrants a year just to keep its pension scheme afloat. Meanwhile in Canada, the Century Initiative, a powerful lobbying group including politicians and at least one former prime minister, aims to increase the country's population from 40 million to 100 million by the end of the century, almost entirely through mass immigration.

One major irony of Western governments' reliance on replacement migration is that the populations being brought to the West to replace native populations are suffering from exactly the same fertility problems. According to new research published by Professor Shanna Swan and others, men in Latin America, Asia, and Africa are suffering the same precipitous declines in total sperm counts and concentrations as Western men.[90] What's more, the declines seem to have been accelerating globally since the year 2000.

Don't think this means Western governments will stop importing millions of foreigners to sustain population growth. The non-Western world contains at least 7/8th of the world's population, so Western governments will be able to continue swamping their countries with migrants even as global fertility rates plummet further.

Nationalist Solutions

CONSERVATIVE AND right-wing governments that want to do something about falling birth rates without relying on mass immigration are going to have to take exposure to harmful chemicals seriously. Hungary's prime minister Viktor Orbán has been feted and vilified for his attempts to increase his country's birth rate by encouraging young Hungarians to breed with each other. Young couples are now offered interest-free loans that will be canceled once they start having children, and women who have four or more children are exempt from income tax for life. In doing so, Orbán is emulating the attempts of the first Roman Emperor, Augustus, with his *leges Juliae*, which provided a mix of financial incentives and social and legal punishments to encourage procreation among the Roman elite. "We do not need numbers," Orbán said in 2019, "We need *Hungarian* children."

When Orbán announced the loans and tax breaks in 2019, Hungary's population was falling by 32,000 a year. The country's birth rate has now increased by 25 percent, from a dismal 1.23 per family in 2010, the lowest in the EU, to 1.59 in 2021. That's a significant leap in a short period of time, of course, but it's well short of a replacement birth rate—the level of births needed to ensure the population increases—which would be around 2.1.

It's hard to know, however, if the bounce since 2010 was caused by Orbán and his laws and incentives or by the recovery of the Hungarian economy after the financial crisis of 2008. Hungary was one of the worst-hit nations in the EU. Other countries in the region were also hit badly by the crash and have since experienced a similar revival in birth rates, without any of Orbán's pro-natal measures. Historically, there's little reason to believe a society can legislate its way out of a fertility crisis. There's no evidence that Augustus's *leges Juliae* really worked. A hundred years later, the Roman historian Tacitus was still complaining about the exact same problems: the barrenness of Roman women by comparison with the ancient Germans, the general air of moral decay, the celebration of adultery, and the lucrative practice of inheritance-hunting. The Hungarian birth rate is now falling again, although the pandemic may explain this. Only time will tell.

As I've shown, the causes of precipitous fertility decline go well beyond the social, cultural, and financial. It's not simply that people are encouraged not to have babies by the prevailing culture and that young people are hard-pressed economically to afford it. The biological conditions of the modern world, and our short-sighted pollution of the entire biosphere, are making it more and more difficult for creatures of all kinds to reproduce.

But exposure to endocrine disruptors could be doing even more than that. The effects of endocrine disruptors go beyond just making it harder to reproduce. These chemicals are inverting the very genders themselves, causing profound gender confusion—gender dysphoria and ultimately transgenderism, aided by surgical and hormonal interventions—that threatens to undo the very notion of biological sex itself.

One man warned us about this, and we didn't listen. Alex Jones.

CHAPTER 4

The Gay Frogs Come Home to Roost

"The option isn't even open to us, thanks to the criminal inadequacy of biomedical research in this area. If the choice now is either such additives or catastrophe, we shall have catastrophe. It might be possible to develop such population control tools, although the task would not be simple. Either the additive would have to operate equally well and with minimum side effects against both sexes, or some way would have to be found to direct it only to one sex and shield the other. Feeding potent male hormones to the whole population might sterilize and defeminize the women, while the upset in the male population and society as a whole can be well imagined."

—PAUL R. EHRLICH, *The Population Bomb* (1968)

"I DON'T LIKE 'EM PUTTING CHEMICALS IN THE WATER THAT TURN THE FRIGGIN' FROGS GAY!"

—ALEX JONES, *INFOWARS* live broadcast (2015)

— ♦♦♦ —

How Alex Jones Was Right All Along

IN 2009, biologist Tyrone B. Hayes and a group of fellow biologists from the University of California, Berkeley conducted an experiment involving African clawed frogs and the herbicide atrazine.[91] Hayes and his colleagues exposed male clawed frog larvae to the herbicide and observed the effects on their development into adult frogs, including changes to their genitalia, reproductive parameters such as testosterone levels and sperm count, and their

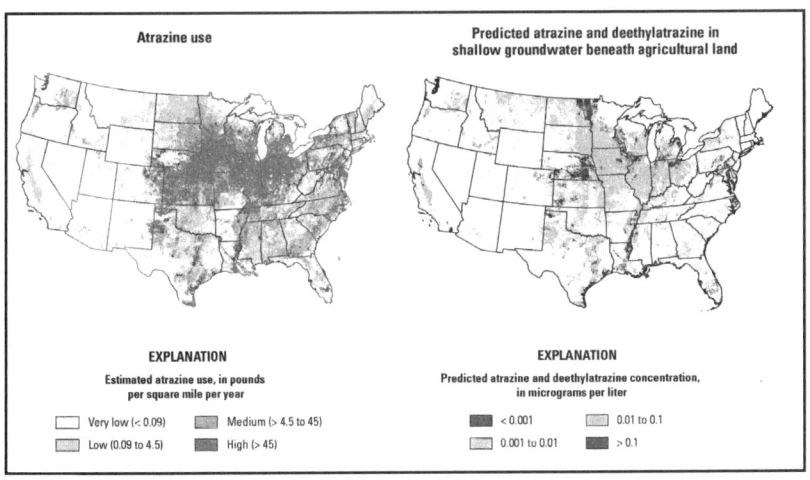

THE QUALITY OF OUR NATION'S WATERS—WATER QUALITY IN PRINCIPAL AQUIFERS OF THE UNITED STATES, 1991–2010: U.S. GEOLOGICAL SURVEY CIRCULAR 1360, 151 P.[92]

sexual behavior in relation to female clawed frogs and other males.

Atrazine was chosen because it's one of the most popular herbicides in the world, sprayed on everything from the endless corn and soy fields of the American Midwest to school football fields and local golf courses. As a result, atrazine is among the most persistent environmental pollutants there is. In the United States, atrazine is a chemical that's almost impossible to avoid contact with, whether you're a human or a little frog in a pond somewhere sitting on a log.

> Approximately 80 million pounds are applied annually in the United States alone, and atrazine is the most common pesticide contaminant of ground and surface water. Atrazine can be transported more than 1,000 km from the point of application via rainfall and, as a result, contaminates otherwise pristine habitats, even in remote areas where it is not used. In fact, more than a half million pounds of atrazine are precipitated in rainfall each year in the United States.[93]

These are important points to remember about chemical pollutants like herbicides and pesticides and fire retardants and plasticizers: they don't just remain where they're sprayed, but travel vast distances and befoul areas far from where they're first applied. Blood and tissue samples from the Inuit of the Arctic Circle consistently record shockingly high levels of chemicals like PFAS and polychlorinated biphenyls, not because the Inuit have suddenly abandoned subsistence hunting and gone all-in on heavy industry, but because weather patterns and the large mammals and fish they feed on carry the chemicals there over many thousands of miles.

What's also notable about atrazine is that it's a vicious endocrine disruptor, a class of chemicals we encountered in the last chapter. As we saw, endocrine disruptors alter the body's natural balance of hormones, with potentially terrible consequences for our health and the health of the animal world. By the time of the 2009 experiment, it was well established that atrazine induces a wide range of endocrine-disrupting effects on animals and in human in-vitro studies, and these are also laid out at length by Hayes and his colleagues:

> In addition to its persistence, mobility, and widespread contamination of water, atrazine is also a concern because several studies have shown that atrazine is a potent endocrine disruptor active in the ppb (parts per billion) range in fish, amphibians, reptiles, and human cell lines, and at higher doses (ppm) in reptiles, birds, and laboratory rodents. Atrazine seems to be most potent in amphibians, where it is active at levels as low as 0.1 ppb. Although a few studies suggest that atrazine has no effect on amphibians under certain laboratory conditions, in other studies, atrazine reduces testicular volume; reduces germ cell and Sertoli cell numbers [reproductive cells in the testes]; induces hermaphroditism; reduces testosterone; and induces testicular oogenesis [the development of female gametes, i.e. eggs]. Furthermore, atrazine contamination is associated with demasculinization and feminization of amphibians in agricultural areas where atrazine is used and directly correlated with atrazine contamination in the wild.[94]

Hayes and his team had been researching the effects of atrazine on amphibian life for the better part of a decade by this point, beginning in 2002 with a study that confirmed anecdotal reports atrazine was disrupting the testicular development of wild male frogs.[95] The team had already published at least four scientific papers on the subject.

In their 2009 experiment, Hayes et al. showed that, even at low doses commonly found in the wider environment, atrazine was potent enough to induce catastrophic reproductive effects in clawed frogs.

"Atrazine-exposed males were both demasculinized (chemically castrated) and completely feminized as adults," the study explains. These unfortunate frogs suffered reduced testosterone levels, their reproductive organs were smaller, they produced fewer sperm and were less fertile, and they generally engaged in less mating behavior. Eighty percent of the male frogs were unable to produce any sperm at all. Even more worryingly, a full 10 percent of the male larvae exposed to atrazine changed their gender. They developed into "functional females" that not only had sex with male clawed frogs that hadn't been exposed to atrazine but were also able to produce "viable" eggs. For all intents and purposes, these frogs that had started life as male embryos were now female.

Atrazine, the most popular herbicide in America—that stuff you spray on your lawn—is making male frogs change their gender and mate with other male frogs.

In short, there are chemicals in the environment, including the water, that turn the frogs gay.

The Coming of the Gay Frogs

LAUGH ALL you want: the study was taken in deadly seriousness and widely reported as soon as it was released. There was coverage from *Scientific American, Reuters,* and *National Geographic,* among others. "Weed Killer Makes Male Frogs Lay Eggs," ran the *National Geographic* headline.[96] "The so-called pregnant man has company," the report began, a reference to Thomas Beatie, a female-to-male transgender who caused a sensation in the mid-noughties when "he" gave birth after undergoing gender reassignment surgery. Beatie has now given birth to three children, all while still remaining a "man." After outlining the study's findings and interviewing lead author Hayes, the report ends with a section on possible "human impacts."

"Though there haven't been many studies on the chemicals' impacts on people, some recent research has linked atrazine exposure to breast cancer," the report notes. "The U.S. Environmental Protection Agency recently announced it's reevaluating atrazine—banned in the European Union since 2004—to determine possible harmful effects to people."[97]

It's worth noting the complete lack of contention and hostility that greeted the study. There weren't regime-appointed fact-checkers back in 2010, at least not like today, and chemical castration and the even stronger possibility of chemicals causing transgenderism hadn't become a "culture war" issue in the way it would just a few years later. Of course, there were some who disputed the study's findings, as they'd disputed earlier work on the subject. Not least among them, unsurprisingly, was Syngenta, the Swiss manufacturer of atrazine. Even today, despite a litany of studies on atrazine's harmful effects, Syngenta's website states that "atrazine is effective, safe and integral to the success of agriculture in the United States and worldwide."[98]

What it took to make atrazine-induced feminization a "culture war" issue was one man, Alex Emmerich Jones, the founder and host of INFOWARS—and the mainstream media's hatred of him.

The Conspiracy Theory That Isn't

IT'S NOW been nine years since Alex Jones unleashed his "gay frogs" rant on the world, guaranteeing for himself a place in the annals of meme history and also inadvertently helping to make the issue of endocrine-disruptors and their feminizing effects a "dangerous right-wing conspiracy theory." On the day of that fateful rant, Jones was talking about secret government plans to create a "gay bomb" that would feminize the male population and reduce the birth rate dramatically.

"What do you think tap water is? It's a gay bomb, baby," he said with poise—before exploding.

"I DON'T LIKE 'EM PUTTING CHEMICALS IN THE WATER THAT TURN THE FRIGGIN' FROGS GAY! DO YOU UNDERSTAND THAT?"

Jones then smashed the table with his fist, sending his assorted papers flying. "AARGH! CRAP!" he bellowed. Rant over.

But it was just the beginning.

That wasn't the first time Jones had brought up the link between feminization and toxic chemicals, but it was the most attention-grabbing by far. Five years earlier, for example, he had suggested the government was deliberately putting estrogenic chemicals in the water and in consumer products such as beverage cans and processed food.

Secret population control—the claim that governments and shadowy figures have been putting harmful chemicals in the food and water supply to sterilize people and reduce the global population—was already, in a real sense, the ur-"conspiracy theory." This was something that had been talked about for many decades—for as long as globalist movers and shakers like Julian Huxley, brother of Aldous, and Bertrand Russell and Paul Ehrlich had been writing about controlling the population by such devious means—but the "gay frogs" rant made it an Alex Jones signature. Now, along with the false flag and especially the fake school-shooting, this was a "theory" that would forever be associated personally with the big man from Austin, Texas, and his alternative-media empire, INFOWARS.

Within a short period of time, it became simply impossible to talk about issues and ask questions that a few years earlier had been considered politically nonpartisan in respected magazines and journals like *National Geographic* and *Scientific American*. This coincided with the broader demonization of Alex Jones, ostensibly for his role in denying that the Sandy Hook shooting took place, but really for his pivotal role in helping Donald Trump get elected in 2016. Virtually all the key figures in securing Trump's historic win have now been punished by the regime in one way or another—slander and defamation, prosecution and endless lawfare, bankruptcy, or usually some combination of all of those things. Everyone from big beasts like Steve Bannon, Roger Stone, and General Michael Flynn, to humble "shitposters" like Douglass Mackey. Mackey, the man behind the "Ricky Vaughn" Twitter account, posted hot takes and memes mocking Hillary Clinton during the 2016 election, and for that "crime" was arrested five years later, just days after Biden took office in 2021.[99] At time of writing, Mackey is appealing his conviction for voter suppression under a statute brought in during Reconstruction to counter the Ku Klux Klan and its assaults on newly enfranchised blacks in the South.

Jones didn't help his credibility, of course, by dressing as a gay frog in the weeks after the rant.[100] A video excerpt of the rant had already gone viral on Twitter, and the hashtag #gayfrogs was trending. The rant even became an indie song. Never one to let a good controversy go to waste, Jones decided to appear on his show in a full frog bodysuit and pink frilly tutu, his face painted green. "Thanks to atrazine there will be no more frogs, but we are gay so that's cool," simpered Alex

Jones the homosexual amphibian, as he drank from a bottle labeled "atrazine." "I'll never have children and I'm sterilized, but the media says I'm totally cool. I'm a gay frog!"

The "Far Right" and the "Greening of Hate"

AND SO it was that the "gay frogs" rant became just another deranged, dangerous thing in a litany of deranged, dangerous things that Alex Jones has said. Scarcely worth a moment's consideration. And if it is worth consideration, only as an example of the twisted delusions conjured by hateful "white supremacists" and members of the "alt right" and "far right" as they impotently rage against the modern world. Since 2015, there's been a slew of articles with titles like "White Genocide and Male Extinction in the Rhetoric of Endocrine Disruptors"—yes, that's a real title[101]—and "Theorizing the Gay Frog"—yes, that's real too[102]—that try to convince us that fears about the effects of exposure to chemicals like atrazine are rooted in genuinely fictitious concepts like "white extinction anxiety." In case you didn't know, "white extinction anxiety" is the fear that the future of the white race is being imperiled by falling birth rates, shifting demographics, and the political changes that follow in their wake. This represents a "greening of hate . . . in which concern for the environment is co-opted as a ruse for increased control over women's reproductive capacities, surveillance of racial minorities, and securing the borders against immigration."[103]

What a tremendous shame, for a number of reasons. Not least of all, because it was the opposite of Jones's intention. Jones deserves enormous credit for being one of the first figures in all media—left and right, alternative and mainstream—to raise awareness of the terrible, pervasive effects of industrial and agricultural pollution. Alex Jones was many people's first introduction to atrazine and glyphosate and the idea that industrial chemicals could mimic the effects of natural hormones in our bodies, with terrible consequences. He deserves a debt of gratitude for this, whether you like him or not.

The bigger tragedy, of course, is that we've been prevented from talking about this for almost a decade, during which time the problem has only gotten worse. Our exposure to endocrine disruptors and harmful chemicals has almost certainly increased—the world isn't using less plastic or fewer industrial chemicals: it's using more, much more—and gender dysphoria and transgenderism have increased too.

The Rise in Gender Dysphoria

A STUDY published in 2023 showed a massive growth in the prevalence of gender dysphoria across the period from 2017 to 2022.[104] Using the data of 42 million people aged between four and 65, 80 percent of whom were living in America, researchers found that 66,078 people were diagnosed with gender dysphoria, equivalent to a rate of 155 people per 100,000.

The mean age of diagnosis also plummeted 15 percent, from 31 years old to 26. This was more notable for females than males. Among females, there has been a sharp acceleration of diagnoses before the age of twenty-two. The number of diagnoses rose sharply at age eleven, peaked between seventeen and nineteen, and then fell below the figure for males at age twenty-two. For males, by contrast, the prevalence of diagnoses began to increase noticeably after the age of thirteen, reaching its height at twenty-three, before gradually decreasing.

This new incidence figure is far higher than other numbers in the scientific literature. A study covering the Netherlands for a period from 1972 to 2015 assessed the prevalence in 2015 as around thirty-six per 100,000 people for men and nineteen per 100,000 for women.[105] Worldwide meta-analyses covering Europe, America, and Australia over the same period have placed the figure even lower: 4.6 per 100,000, in one study.[106]

It's worth noting that there are difficulties with the statistics, including questions about diagnostic criteria, methods of assessment, and terminology used. Do we include people who say they've questioned their gender or do we only include people who meet the medical definition of suffering gender dysphoria? Do we restrict ourselves to people who've been medically diagnosed with gender dysphoria? Or do we go even further and only consider people who've

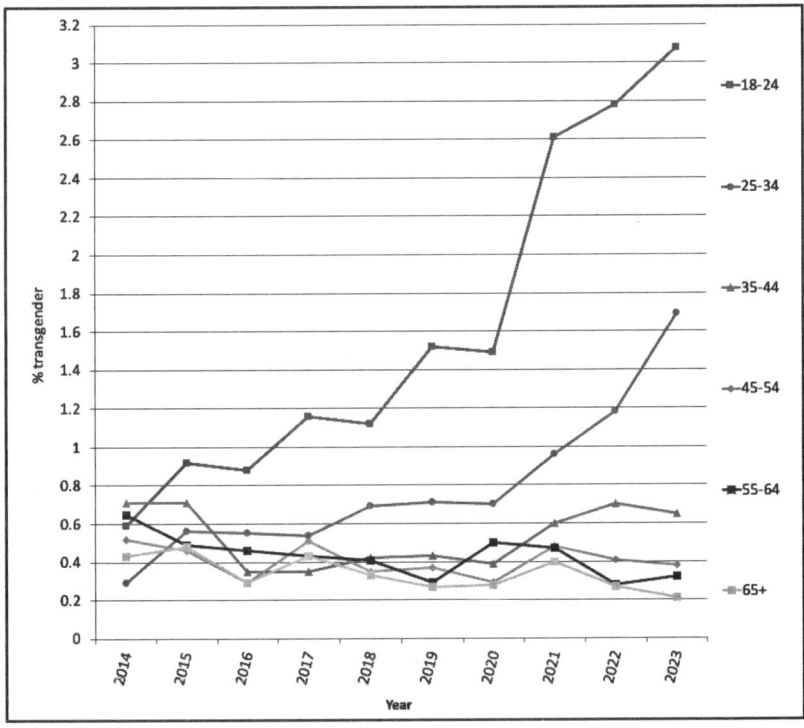

INCREASES IN SELF-IDENTIFYING AS TRANSGENDER AMONG US ADULTS, 2014–2022. SEXUALITY RESEARCH AND SOCIAL POLICY. 1–19. 10.1007/S13178-024-01001-7 [107]

undergone or are scheduled to undergo hormonal therapy or surgery? These are valid questions, and they affect the answers we get and the comparability of data.

Our general perception, shaped and determined by the mainstream media and cultural and political programmers, is of course that transgenderism or "gender fluidity" or whatever you want to call it, is on the rise. Just look around you. It's everywhere. And, of course, it's presented as a wonderful thing: to be celebrated, embraced, and even emulated. It's hard not to have a nagging feeling that the visibility of transgenderism, the saturation of media with leering drag queens, along with teenagers showing off their mastectomy scars, is just a function of liberalism and its endless quest to push the frontiers of "liberation" yet further. An alien visitor to Britain or any other Western country today, watching the television or scrolling ads on the internet, would think every young couple consisted of a black man and a white woman, although interracial relationships still remain a vanishingly small proportion of relationships, and in-group preference is the norm. But even so, the most rigorous studies, including a Swedish report and analysis published in *Nature* that covers the period 2001 to 2016, have shown significant increases in gender dysphoria in recent years, and they also provide good reason to believe other studies have underestimated this condition in all its forms.[108]

Another Front in the Culture War

EXPLANATIONS THAT treat this rise as anything other than a sincere phenomenon, as something more than people finally being able to throw off the shackles of social and cultural conditioning and express themselves as *who they really are*, are generally subject to intense dispute and anger. Transgenderism is now *the* "culture war" issue, the barometer of whether a society is truly progressive and truly stands for the new holy trinity of diversity, inclusivity and equity. You're either for transgenderism, in which case you're good—an "ally" if you don't have the special fortune to be transgender yourself—or you're against it, in which case you're everything from a "transphobe" up to and including a Nazi or even Adolf Hitler himself. Despite the opprobrium, the persecution under absurd and tyrannical "hate speech" laws, and the physical threats and attacks that have now become routine methods of disciplining and silencing "gender-critical" people, there are scholars who refuse to be cowed, and instead bravely continue to investigate associations between social and psychological factors on the one hand, and gender dysphoria and transgenderism on the other.

A 2018 study in the journal *PLoS One*, for example, showed that increased social media use and having friends who've already been diagnosed with gender dysphoria are clear factors in the onset of new cases among young people.[109] This is transgenderism-as-social-contagion. It suggests, quite clearly, that transgenderism, especially among children and teenagers, has a clear continuity with other crazes like anorexia and bulimia, self-harm, and glue-sniffing. The rise of mental illness has also been implicated. A 2014 study showed that nearly 63 percent of sampled patients who requested gender-reassignment surgery had "at least one psychiatric comorbidity," with almost a third suffering from depression.[110]

Environmental Explanations: Now Is the Time

WHEN IT comes to environmental and chemical explanations of gender dysphoria, however, it's still early days. Very early days. As I noted in an article on the subject back in 2023, if you go on one of the large online databases of scientific articles and search for, say, "endocrine disruptors transgenderism" or "endocrine disruptors gender dysphoria," you'll get more or less zero hits.[111]

The general atmosphere is more receptive to such work than it once was, however. Alex Jones remains as polarizing a figure as he's ever been, but the events of the pandemic have validated large aspects of his worldview and predictions, and the depth of his persecution over Sandy Hook, including a $1 billion settlement with the families, has generated outrage and sympathy in equal measure. Endocrine disruptors are now a political talking point, and the link with transgenderism has been given a renewed legitimacy by the appearance of Robert F. Kennedy Jr. as a presidential candidate and then incoming Secretary of the U.S. Department of Health and Human Services. In an essay for *The American Mind*,[112] I even suggested that the 2024 election would be the "gay frogs" election, as a riff on Michael Anton's "Flight 93 election" article back in 2016.[113] Don't let the humorous intention fool you, though. It's a big thing for a presidential candidate to be talking like RFK Jr.

In a podcast appearance with Jordan Peterson after his announcement, RFK Jr. carefully linked the explosion in gender dysphoria to our increasing exposure to endocrine-disrupting chemicals, and he explicitly referred to the Hayes clawed-frog study. The podcast was removed from YouTube for an unspecified terms-of-service violation, but RFK Jr. repeated the claim in a three-hour podcast with Joe Rogan that managed to avoid being taken down. There was open pushback in the mainstream media, of course. "RFK Jr. says trans frog prove chemicals in the water are turning kids trans: The Dem. Presidential hopeful's crackpot theory, involving male frogs turning into 'viable females,' is literally right out of 'Jurassic Park'"—that was the headline on website LGBTQ Nation.[114] *Newsweek*, CNN, *PolitiFact*, *TheWrap*, MSN, and pretty much every mainstream media outlet ran some kind of denunciation of RFK Jr. and his resurrection of the "gay frogs" theory. But it's clear the terms of the debate have changed. RFK Jr. is not Alex Jones. Alex Jones was not running for president—nor likely to become a member of the Cabinet in the U.S. government. Yet.

Perhaps the most surprising effect was on Donald Trump, whose idea of a "presidential commission into chronic disease" could only have been a response to RFK Jr. announcing his candidacy, with its clear health-based focus. "In recent decades, there has been an unexplained and alarming growth in the prevalence of chronic illnesses and health problems, especially in children," the former president said in a video released on Rumble. "We've seen a stunning rise in autism, auto-immune disorders, obesity, infertility, serious allergies, and respiratory challenges. It is time to ask, 'What is going on?'"[115] It could almost have been RFK Jr. speaking and not Donald Trump. Trump sounded particularly Kennedy-esque when he said that Big Pharma is too close to regulators and public-health institutions, and that government money would be better spent finding and addressing the underlying causes of ill health, rather than paying for ad-hoc treatments.

Covert Population Control?

THERE ARE also promising new leads from scientists that establish the "gay frogs" theory on a new footing. Let's discuss those studies in detail. But first, I want to consider the other "strong" aspect of Alex Jones's "gay frogs" claim: that endocrine-disrupting chemicals are added to the food and water supply *deliberately* for the purposes of population control. Do we have any actual evidence for this, apart from the longstanding desire of people like Paul Ehrlich—stated quite openly in the quote at the head of the chapter—to do it?

My general position is that we have ended up bathed in harmful chemicals, unable to avoid exposure to them even in the most remote parts of the planet, through happenstance and the wrong attitude to risk. Corporate greed plays a part too—a big part. This pollution is a feature of our modern world, not a glitch—especially our reliance on plastics. We live in a plastic world. Our world as it is now would not only be inconceivable without plastic and its miraculous physical properties, it would be impossible. And plastics and plastic chemicals are almost all endocrine disruptors in one form or another. Or, at least, the chemicals we know about are. Because in reality we know very little about the thousands, even tens of thousands, of chemicals involved in the production of plastics.

A project called the Plastic Health Map illustrates this point well.[116] Since the 1960s, there have been thousands of studies of plastics and their effects on animals and humans, but nobody had ever thought to catalog them in order to provide a comprehensive profile of the risks. Researchers at the Minderoo Foundation decided to do exactly that: to create a searchable database of plastic studies that allows complex cross-referencing on the basis of different variables, such as the type of chemical, its health effects, the age of the research subjects involved, and the year of publication.

Experts believe there may be as many as 13,000 different chemicals involved in the manufacture of plastics today. Investigating over 10,000 chemicals would have been beyond the capabilities of the researchers at the Minderoo Foundation, so instead they decided to take a subset of 1,500 chemicals, including familiar ones like bisphenols, per- and polyfluoroalkyl substances (PFAS), flame retardants, and phthalates, as well as others that are far less well known. The researchers were then able to identify a total of around 3,500 studies of plastic chemicals and their effects on living creatures published between 1960 and 2022.

What they discovered is that those 3,500 studies accounted for just 30 percent of the total number of chemicals they had sampled. Seventy percent had no safety data whatsoever. Nothing. That's over 1,000 chemicals out of a total of 1,500. Extrapolated to 13,000 chemicals, that's over 9,000 with no safety data at all.

Happenstance. And also folly. We have proceeded too far, too fast, without fully understanding the nature of the substances that sustain this brave new world we live in. Our attitude to novel chemicals, whether they be plasticizers or food additives, has (broadly speaking) been one of "safe until proven otherwise." Although there may be some safety testing before new chemicals are introduced, it's short-term and easily manipulated in the interests of commerce. We can't test new chemicals on humans, of course, and so instead we rely on animal proxies and then do the real long-term human testing on consumers. Only then do we start to find the long-term effects. But by that time, years or even decades after the introduction of a new chemical, there are entrenched financial interests working against regulation. Furthermore, recognition of causality—and therefore assignment of blame—is much more diffuse and difficult to identify than in tightly controlled laboratory conditions.

Who Watches the Watchmen?

THE ATTITUDE of "safe until proven otherwise" leads to a ridiculous situation where, even when harmful chemicals are eventually identified and then regulated or banned, replacements are introduced that turn out to be as harmful as, if not worse than, the chemicals they replaced. This is true, for example, of the various chemicals that have been brought in to replace bisphenol A, like bisphenol S—which is why you should avoid "BPA-free" water bottles and food preparation and storage equipment. It's also true of "safe" alternatives to phthalates, like acetyl tributyl citrate (ATBC), which was recently shown to impair neural development, with the possibility that maternal exposure may cause brain damage in babies.[117]

When it comes to food additives, the U.S. system, under the management of the FDA, is a beacon of stupidity. I've described the FDA's "Generally Recognized as Safe" (GRAS) system as "Generally Recognized as Insane" for the cavalier attitude to novel ingredients it licenses.[118] The system was first introduced in 1958, when the Food Additive Amendments were passed, to require that all non-standard food additives—the kind of things that aren't typically found in a normal kitchen—should be tested adequately for safety in humans.

When the new system was introduced, there were reckoned to be about 700 food additives in use, 400 of which were thought to be safe in the long term. The new system was supposed to make sure additives that were already in the food supply were safe, but what happened instead was a process of "grandfathering," where substances that were already in use were simply assumed to be safe for that very reason. That included substances like potassium bromate, which over 50 years' worth of research has shown to be linked to cancers such as thyroid and testicular cancer, kidney damage, gut dysbiosis, and reproductive issues. The EU, Canada, China, and India have now banned it. Even Nigeria has banned it. But not the U.S.

Around 2,000 additives are licensed for use in the EU. In the U.S., the figure rises to 10,000—and that's just an estimate. In truth, nobody really knows how many additives are in the food supply, not even the FDA, because companies are simply introducing additives without telling anybody. A company can produce a new food additive, decide it's safe and then bring it to market without any scrutiny from the FDA at all. How did this happen?

When companies first started applying for GRAS designation, they were allowed to submit their own safety data for their novel ingredients, which the FDA could then choose to accept or reject. But as a huge backlog of applications began to build up at the FDA, companies started adding novel ingredients to their products without any consultation with the FDA at all. The FDA could have asserted its authority, but it did what any poorly staffed, totally compromised institution like the FDA would do: It simply made the problem disappear by defining it out of existence. The FDA retrospectively normalized the situation, a process it completed in 2016.

The commercial incentives for such a system are obvious. If you were a company executive, of course you'd prefer not to wait years before your new chemical, which is essential to make your latest product, could be introduced. Matters aren't helped by the fact that there's basically zero independence between regulatory bodies like the FDA and the companies they're supposed to regulate. An investigation by *The British Medical Journal* in 2023, for example, showed that two regulators who approved Moderna's mRNA COVID vaccine went to work for the company within months of leaving the FDA.[119] A 2018 investigation by *Science* magazine found "11 of 16 FDA medical examiners who worked on 28 drug approvals and then left the agency for new jobs are now employed by or consult for the companies they recently regulated. This can create at least the appearance of conflicts of interest."[120]

> Jeffrey Siegel, who was an FDA staff member specializing in reviews for arthritis drugs, oversaw the 2010 approval of Genentech's arthritis drug tocilizumab (Actemra). Months later, he left the agency to join the company and its parent, Roche, as director of the division that includes Actemra and related offerings. Siegel represented Roche before his former FDA colleagues when the company sought approval to promote Actemra for new conditions. Last year, he told STAT [a health website] that the timing of his decision to join Roche and Genentech was coincidental.[121]

I'd say that's more than an "appearance of conflicts of interest."

Who watches the watchmen, indeed?

One of the things the researchers behind the Plastic Health Map call for is a rethink of the way plastic chemicals are licensed. But the truth is, we need a total rethink across the board about a lot more than licensing. And not just for plastic chemicals but *all* novel chemicals, including food additives. The attitude of "safe until proven otherwise" needs to die if we are to have any chance of truly being in control of the chemicals we are exposed to and understanding their effects. "Harmful until proven otherwise" should be the watchword.

Corporate Lies and Government Collusion

AND YET. Revelations in the ongoing PFAS scandal involving DuPont and 3M show that there is more than an element of wilfulness, and even deliberate malice, in the massive pollution of our environment and food supply with toxic chemicals. This may not be systematic population control of the type described by Paul Ehrlich, but it comes close enough. The difference between a sin of omission and a sin of commission is a hair's breadth, if that.

PFAS are a broad class of chemicals with endocrine-disrupting, obesogenic, and carcinogenic effects, and, like so many of these chemicals, they are ubiquitous—everywhere. As documents obtained in lawsuits reveal, DuPont and 3M were both fully aware for nearly half a century that their PFAS chemicals are hugely toxic, even fatal, to animals and humans, long before their toxicity was independently established. Instead of telling regulators by sharing internal company data, they hid this fact for decades.

A study published in 2023 makes clear the horrifying scale of the deception.

> DuPont had evidence of PFAS toxicity from internal animal and occupational studies that they did not publish in the scientific literature and failed to report their findings to EPA as required under TSCA. These documents were all marked as "confidential," and in some cases, industry executives are explicit that they "wanted this memo destroyed."[122]

In 1961, for example, a DuPont internal report stated that Teflon, a PFAS chemical, had "the ability to increase the size of the liver in rats at low doses" and needed to be handled "with extreme care," avoiding all contact with the skin. (That's the Teflon that coats your non-stick frying pan: throw it out now.) In 1970, another report from the DuPont-funded Haskell laboratory noted that the PFAS compound C-8 "was highly toxic when inhaled and moderately toxic when ingested."

In 1980, there were reports of birth defects among the children of female employees working with C-8. DuPont lied to its employees and to regulators, telling them that C-8 "has a lower toxicity, like table salt." In 1991, the company simply brushed off reports of groundwater contamination near a C-8 factory: "C-8 has no known toxic or ill health effects in humans at concentration levels detected."

Lie after lie after lie.

By the early 2000s, the toxicity of PFAS compounds had been established by scientists, with no help from DuPont or 3M or any other manufacturer, and a slew of lawsuits and damaging media attention followed. DuPont took one last roll of the dice. A company executive emailed the EPA and tried to call in a favor.

> "We need EPA to quickly (like first thing tomorrow) say the following: That consumer products sold under the Teflon brand are safe and to date there are no human health effects known to be caused by PFOA [a type of PFAS]."

But the game was up. The EPA eventually fined DuPont $16.5 million for its negligence with regard to PFOA. At the time, it was the largest civil penalty paid under U.S. environmental statutes, but it hardly left a dent in the one billion dollars of PFAS profits DuPont made that year.

This is corporate evil at its archetypal worst. DuPont and 3M aren't names to conjure with like Monsanto, Google, or Walmart—or fictional names like Buy n Large, Omnicorp or Weyland-Yutani—but they just as surely deserve a place in the same pantheon of corporate god-complexes.

We're the Gay Frogs Now

SO WHAT of the other part of the "gay frogs" claim: the link to the rise of transgenderism in humans? Let's take a look at two important recent studies. The second, in particular, is a real bombshell.

A 2022 study in the journal *Psychological Science* shows that low exposure to gonadal hormones—i.e., testosterone and other masculinizing hormones—during gestation and infancy predicts a higher risk of childhood gender nonconformity among boys.[123] Basically, if you're born a biological boy and you don't get enough masculinizing hormones in the very early stages of life, you're more likely to behave in ways that are not typical of boys.

The researchers took 65 men with idiopathic hypogonadotropic hypogonadism ("IHH"), a rare endocrine disorder that affects about 1 in 130,000 live births. These men would have been exposed to low levels of testosterone, maybe even no testosterone at all, from around the second trimester of gestation (weeks thirteen to twenty-eight) until they started hormone replacement therapy, probably at the age of about nineteen. As one of the study authors explains, "Men with IHH are unambiguously male at birth and raised as boys, almost always without their condition being known until the typical time of puberty."

The researchers also looked at thirty-two women with the same condition (i.e., low to zero testosterone) and 437 men and 1,207 women who developed normally.

Participants were given a questionnaire about their childhood behavior and the degree to which they conformed to gender stereotypes: what gender were their friends, what kind of toys did they play with, did they feel satisfied with their gender, did they have fantasies about being another gender, and so on. As it turned out, men with IHH reported significantly less gender conformity than men who developed normally. That meant men with IHH were much more likely to recall preferring female friends, playing with makeup and jewelry, wearing girls' clothes, and feeling less masculine and generally less satisfied with being a boy than other men did.

Another key finding was that women with the condition did not report gender non-conformity as children. What this clearly establishes is that, in the case of men, it's testosterone that's governing normal development towards typical male behaviors and a male sense of self.

This comparison also shows, crucially, that socialization is not a deciding factor, since girls with the condition are raised as girls, as normal, without the same problems. "People who were exposed to different levels of testosterone during their early development are likely to differ in their psychology and behavior even if they are socialized in the same way," the same study author says.

Now, of course, this isn't *direct* evidence that endocrine disruptors are causing gender dysphoria and transgenderism. What it does is help establish, in a strong way, the *prima facie* case for that being so, which goes like this:

1. Exposure to testosterone in utero and during childhood is essential to ensure proper masculine development in boys. Boys who are exposed to reduced levels of testosterone are more likely to experience gender dysphoria, which in many cases leads them to transition.

2. Exposure to a wide variety of endocrine disruptors reduces testosterone and increases estrogen in boys.

3. Exposure to endocrine disruptors happens at every stage of life, from pregnancy onwards.

4. Exposure to endocrine disruptors therefore must be contributing to gender dysphoria and transgenderism.

The First Direct Evidence

THANKFULLY, WE now have another study that does provide direct evidence linking exposure to endocrine disruptors to gender dysphoria and transgenderism.[124] This is the bombshell I mentioned.

I discovered this study early on in 2024 and grasped its significance straight away. It prompted, for example, a piece called "Alex Jones Was Right," for *American Greatness*,[125] to explain the study and why Alex Jones is deserved an apology by his critics and detractors.

The study, published in the *Journal of Xenobiotics*, considers the effects of exposure to the chemical diethylstilbestrol (DES) on the rate of transgenderism among French boys. The results show that boys exposed to DES in utero were as much as 100 times more likely to become male-to-female transgender than the highest reported background rate in Europe. And since reliable figures for the number of transgender people as a percentage of the population vary wildly, the actual risk increase due to DES exposure could be much, much higher.

DES has been banned in the U.S. since the year 2000, but it was used for decades as a treatment for a range of women's ailments, from vaginitis to menopause symptoms. More importantly, it was given to pregnant women with a history of miscarriage, in order—supposedly—to reduce the risk of further complications. Between 1938 and 1971, approximately four million women in the U.S. were given DES during pregnancy alone. (Other uses for DES included fattening up livestock until it was found to give them cancer and as a form of chemical castration to treat homosexuality, the most famous victim being cryptographer Alan Turing.)

There were early suggestions of negative health effects associated with the use of DES, but it wasn't until the 1970s that comprehensive evidence was presented. It became clear that the drug was causing rare forms of vaginal tumours in girls exposed to it in utero, and so in 1971 the FDA withdrew its approval for use during pregnancy. That didn't stop DES being used as, among other things, an emergency contraceptive or treatment for menopause—or to fatten up cows. In the intervening decades, DES has been linked to serious reproductive abnormalities in both sexes: everything from epididymal cysts, undescended testicles (cryptorchidism) and micropenises in boys, to ectopic pregnancies, miscarriages, premature births, and a variety of cancers, including breast cancer and the rare cancers mentioned above. DES has also been linked to psychological disorders: schizophrenia, bipolarism, eating disorders and suicidal behavior, among others.

Some of these effects are multigenerational and transgenerational. Exposure can have ramifications down and across generations even when just a single generation has been exposed. This is something that's now being observed with a large number of harmful chemicals. For example, the weedkiller glyphosate has been shown to make the great-grandchildren of rats exposed to it become obese, even without direct exposure themselves, as well as reducing fertility parameters and increasing risk of kidney disease.[126] This is yet another reason why the current regime of chemical licensing is wildly insufficient. It fails to take into account the potential for multigenerational and transgenerational effects of exposure, even at low levels. It also means that even when we rid our environment of these chemicals, we'll still be dealing with the consequences for decades to come.

The new study took data from 1,200 French mothers who were given DES while pregnant and their nearly 2,000 offspring. A strength of this study is that it includes children these mothers gave birth to before they were ever prescribed DES. This allows the establishment of a comparable rate of transgenderism between sons born with and without exposure to DES.

And what do the results show? Four of the 253 boys who were exposed in utero became transgender, whereas none of the 148 boys who avoided it did. The numbers may seem small, but it's the rate that's important. The study's authors explain.

> If we consider the highest prevalence of transgender women reported in the literature (1/17,000), the prevalence we observed in our study (1.58 percent) is 10- to 100-fold higher. Moreover, the prevalence of female transgender identity was 0 percent among the 148 elder non-exposed sons in the same informative families.[127]

So there we have it. Exposure to DES in utero as a boy carries perhaps as much as a hundredfold increased risk of becoming transgender.

The size of the study is a limitation, but as I said earlier, millions of American women alone were given DES while pregnant, so there's tremendous potential for large-scale investigations to confirm these findings. And, what's more, DES is just one endocrine-disrupting chemical. There are thousands and thousands more, all of which could be investigated to discover possible relationships with transgenderism. We could have more studies of in utero exposure and lifetime risk of becoming transgender. We could have studies that measure levels of endocrine disruptors in the bodies of people undergoing transition and compare them to levels in people who aren't.

Gay Frogs Are No Longer Hypothetical

THIS IS just the beginning. But what it means, undeniably, is that the "gay frogs" claim is no longer hypothetical. No longer must we make inferences from studies of African clawed frogs or other non-human animals, and no longer do we need to lay out a *prima facie* case and make conclusions by inference.

We can simply say: this study shows that exposure to an endocrine disruptor massively increases the risk of becoming transgender. And the critics and disbelievers must answer that.

So, yes, Alex Jones was right. But now you don't need to invoke his name, which many will still be wary of doing, to say there is a truly non-political, non-partisan mandate to investigate this matter with urgency and with the rigor only genuine science, at its objective best, is able to provide.

This is absolutely the right thing to do. It's not even a threat to transgender people. It's easy, of course, to mock drag queen groomers, to recoil in disgust at their gross parodies of female sexuality, to want to protect children from being preyed upon by sexual deviants consumed by the most transgressive of all desires—to corrupt what is truly innocent, what is most helpless and most in need of the protection of adults—but we also need to remember that many people suffer with the burden of gender dysphoria through no fault of their own. They are products of the modern world and of our peculiar attitude to risk and progress, which has flooded the world with chemicals we still know very little about. These people need sympathy. They need help.

Another strength of this new French study is the fact that it brings to the foreground the stories of some of the French boys who were exposed to DES and how that toxic legacy

113

has shaped their lives. They are allowed to speak in their own words, and their stories are profoundly moving, even if brief. Here's one of them.

> Currently a composer (guitar and vocals), S. was born in 1969 after in-utero exposure to DES. At birth, S. had male genitalia with unilateral cryptorchidism. S. started to question the assigned male gender at the age of 4 years: "I remember very clearly that when I was 3–4 years old, one day I went with my mother to a hairdressing salon and having looked at all the ladies, I thought: 'When I grow up this is what I will do: I will be a woman.'"
>
> During adolescence, S. felt he was a woman and had severe psychological disorders, particularly depression and suicidal ideation . . . As an adult, S. married and had two children. These two girls had prolactinoma [a condition where the body produces too much prolactin, limiting sex-hormone production], and one has Asperger's syndrome, androgyny and ovarian cysts. S. began the transition with male to female gender reassignment surgery, in Brighton, United Kingdom (UK), in November 2015. Since then, S. has been receiving GAHT [hormone therapy] and is followed by the doctor who managed the transition. According to the UK Gender Recognition Act, S. could change their sex recorded on their birth certificate (male to female) and now, she lives in Scotland. Her elder sister, also exposed to DES in utero after her mother's miscarriage, died due to vaginal adenocarcinoma during adolescence.[128]

How could anybody condemn or hate a person who has experienced such compounding tragedy in their life? For the sake of people like S., and to spare others their unfortunate fate, we must pursue the truth, however painful and "politically incorrect" it may be.

However much it may hurt liberal critics to admit Alex Jones was right all along.

CHAPTER 5

The Community of Pigs

"Everything about corn meshes smoothly with the gears of this giant machine; grass doesn't. Grain is the closest thing in nature to an industrial commodity: storable, portable, fungible, ever the same today as it was yesterday and will be tomorrow. Since it can be accumulated and traded, grain is a form of wealth. It is a weapon too . . . The nations with the biggest surpluses of grain have always exerted power over the ones in short supply. Throughout history governments have encouraged their farmers to grow more than enough grain, to protect against famine, to free up labor for other purposes, to improve the trade balance, and generally to augment their power . . . The real beneficiary of this crop is not America's eaters but its military-industrial complex. In an industrial economy, the growing of grain supports the larger economy: the chemical and biotech industries, the oil industry, Detroit, pharmaceuticals (without which they couldn't keep animals healthy in CAFOs), agribusiness, and the balance of trade. Growing corn helps drive the very industrial complex that drives it. No wonder why the government subsidizes it so lavishly."

—MICHAEL POLLAN, *The Omnivore's Dilemma,* p. 210

"Welcome to the year 2030. Welcome to my city—or should I say, 'our city.' I don't own anything. I don't own a car. I don't own a house. I don't own any appliances or any clothes."

—IDA AUKEN, "Welcome to 2030. I Own Nothing, Have No Privacy, and Life Has Never Been Better."

– ♦♦♦ –

117

Processed Food and
Our Plant-Based Future

FOOD AND social control go together like peas and carrots, and they always have done. That was the foundational message of my book, *The Eggs Benedict Option*,[129] which opened with a discussion of an under-appreciated section of Book II of Plato's *Republic*. Vegetarianism has been understood for thousands of years to be an effective means of individual and social control, a means of quieting and keeping at bay man's aggressive, competitive urges, and Plato—or rather, Plato's Socrates—states this fact for the first time in written history, at least as far as we know. There's a reason why for centuries only Buddhist monks regularly ate unfermented soy, a food rich in phytoestrogenic compounds like isoflavones, and it had everything to do with quelling their wayward desires and returning their minds and bodies to the task of total physical self-effacement. Nirvana.

Food and social control: We seem to have forgotten something that should be totally obvious.

There's a tremendous book called *Merchants of Grain*, written in 1979, about the five major companies that controlled the world's wheat supply at that time: Cargill, Continental, Louis Dreyfus, Bunge and André.[130] If you've heard of any of these companies, you've probably only heard of

Cargill. That was certainly true for me when I first read the book. Now, these companies and their control of the global wheat trade might sound like a dull topic for a book, but in fact it's quite the opposite. The book is a fascinating, sometimes shocking, illustration of the importance of a single food crop to everything from diet to U.S. foreign policy in Africa and the Middle East.

> It is difficult to understand how the international grain companies could have slipped through history as inconspicuously as they have. Grain is the only resource in the world that is even more central to modern civilization than oil. It goes without saying that grain is essential to human lives and health. But as much as oil, grain has its politics, its history, its effects on foreign affairs. After World War II, dozens of countries that had once fed themselves began to depend on a distant source—the United States—for a substantial part of their food supply. As America became the center of the planetary food system, trade routes were transformed, new economic relationships took shape, and grain became one of the foundations of the postwar American Empire. Food prices, diets, the dollar, politics and diplomacy were all affected.[131]

Cutting Against the Grain

WHY IS this? Why have we forgotten the importance of grain—and food—when the control of other resources, most of which are less, even far less, crucial to existence, seems so obvious even a child could grasp it?

In the case of the grain companies, some of this is deliberate obfuscation. As the author of *Merchants of Grain*, Dan Morgan, makes clear, companies like Dreyfus and Bunge did their very best to remain out of the public eye and to escape political scrutiny in all forms, mainly through the way they were owned and organized. In 1975, the Senate Subcommittee on Multinational Corporations began investigating the role of grain companies in foreign policy. The brick wall the subcommittee hit was so tall and substantially built, and appeared so quickly in its path, that Senator Frank Church said the following: "No one knows how [the grain companies] operate, what their profits are, what they pay in taxes and what effect they have on our foreign policy—or much of anything else about them."[132] When representatives of Cargill were called before the subcommittee, the company sent a small army of experts who simply "blitzed it," and the questioning was called off after one "bruising" day.

> These "wall-to-wall" witnesses were lined up like a Napoleonic musket regiment going into battle; and they were not content passively to defend themselves but turned the attack back on the subcommittee and accused it of attempting to smear the grain business. Further scheduled hearings were postponed—indefinitely—and there never was any questioning of Continental, Bunge, and the other big companies.[133]

There's more to it than corporate shenanigans. Ernst Jünger said that "long periods of peace and quiet favor certain optical illusions," referring in particular to "the assumption that the invulnerability of the home is founded upon the constitution and safeguarded by it." This is just as true of food. Decades of peace and prosperity mean that a constant supply of all the kinds of food we want to eat is something we take for granted. Food is the basis of our existence, without which there would be no way to live, as surely as if we had no air or water, and yet we just seem to think that it will be there and it doesn't matter where it comes from—by which I mean, who provides it and how. In reality, as the safeguarding of the home rests on the father's willingness to "appear with the axe on the threshold of his dwelling," so the safeguarding of our food rests, ultimately, in our own hands—or it should do.

Food Is Politics

THIS ISN'T an argument for everybody to become subsistence farmers, although in *The Eggs Benedict Option*, I make the case that ordinary people and local communities could produce large quantities of high-quality organic food themselves, in small gardens, if they wanted to, and that this would be one effective way to take back control of the food supply from the corporate players that dominate it and now want to tell us that we must abandon the animal foods we need and love, to save the planet. Here I'm simply putting it to you that who we allow to provide our food is a political question, whether we like it or not and whether we choose to see it or not.

The political nature of food is something we are being forced to confront now, as we're told that in order to prevent catastrophic climate change we must abandon traditional animal agriculture in line with a much broader transformation to the way we live. But, again, there's obfuscation. The language used and the manner in which it is used is simultaneously political but also apolitical or, rather, depoliticized. This is a common ruse of power today. We are encouraged to believe that our response to the "climate crisis" is not really a matter of choice and political action, but an inevitability any "sane" person must face and accept. There's no need for debate or dissent. Can't you see that the planet's boiling? We simply have to get with the program, before it's too late.

But it is a matter of choice and political action. Just ask Plato.

Plato's Community of Pigs: Then and Now

AT THE beginning of Book II of the *Republic*, Socrates and his companions Glaucon and Adeimantus pose an important question: How does justice arise in a community? After the two young men have had their chance to speak at length, Socrates asks them to consider the answer through a metaphor, to think of the development of a city as an allegory for the individual's moral development. The three discuss how a division of labor emerges, how food, shelter, and clothing are provided by different kinds of worker, how the functions of each type of worker complement one another, and how goods are exchanged and sold.

Now the conversation turns to the lifestyle of this imagined community and the kind of foods its people should eat:

> So let us consider first how our citizens, so equipped, will live. They will produce corn, wine, clothes, and shoes, and will build themselves houses. In the summer they will for the most part work unclothed and unshod, in the winter they will be clothed and shod suitably. For food they will prepare wheat-meal or barley-meal for baking or kneading. They will serve splendid cakes and loaves on rushes or fruit leaves, and will sit down to feast with their children on couches of myrtle and bryony; and they will have wine to drink too, and pray to the gods with garlands on their heads, and enjoy each other's company. And fear of poverty and war will make them keep the numbers of their families within their means.[134]

Glaucon objects: "This is pretty plain fare for a feast!" Socrates concedes that the ordinary people should be allowed "a few luxuries," which consist of:

> Salt, of course, and olive oil and cheese, and different kinds of vegetables to make various country dishes. And we must give them some dessert, figs and peas and beans, and myrtle-berries and acorns to roast at the fire as they sip their wine. So they will lead a peaceful and healthy life, and probably die at a ripe old age, bequeathing a similar way of life to their children.

But Glaucon still isn't satisfied. "That's just the fodder you would provide if you were founding a community of pigs!" he says. The people must be allowed to recline on couches, eat off tables, and they should "have the sort of food we have today," by which he means, of course, the meat and fish Socrates would deny them.

Socrates concedes again. Allowing these things might even prove useful for the discussion, he says, but we must remember one thing. While the vegetarian society he has been describing was "the true one, like a man in health," this new society in which people are allowed to eat the flesh of animals is "one in a fever." This social fever will require more than mere "necessaries" to keep in check, and society will become notably more complex as a result. There will have to be new occupations to produce the new goods the people will want. There will also have to be new territory to provide more land for farming as the population increases. And finally, if the neighboring states are also "in a fever," then there will be war, which means a military—a class of "guardians"—is needed.

Here we leave Socrates and his young friends to continue their discussion. What matters so crucially in this brief segment of the *Republic* is what Socrates says, and implies, in his discussion about the most primitive, harmonious form of society. Such a society, just by foregoing meat, is able to keep man's expansionary and self-assertive desires at bay. A society of vegetarians doesn't want more stuff or more land. The inhabitants are content simply to work, to eat and reproduce. Their attitude towards life is a mix of gratitude and fear, especially towards the gods but also the terrible possibility of conflict and war.

Of course, this is ancient Greece, so what Socrates really means is *thymos*. A vegetarian diet is as effective at suppressing *thymos* as any police force. In fact, it's so effective, police aren't even needed. *Thymos*, for our purposes, means testosterone, and in that regard Socrates was certainly right. One study showed that the worst possible diet for maintaining optimal hormone levels is a low-fat vegetarian diet.[135] While a low-fat diet will make a man's testosterone levels fall by an average of 10–15 percent, a low-fat vegetarian diet will by make them plummet by over a quarter, or 26 percent. This is almost certainly because of a lack of key nutrients, and because testosterone levels are correlated with consumption of saturated fat. Saturated fat is one of the building blocks of cholesterol, the sex-hormone precursor, in the body. Research has shown that men who reduce their fat intake from 40 percent of calories with a significant amount of saturated fat to 25 percent of calories with little saturated fat, see a significant decrease in their testosterone.[136] But there are many other reasons beside fat content that plant-based diets are sub-optimal for human, and especially male, health.

Plato's Inheritors: The Great Reset

TODAY'S SOCIAL planners, the inheritors of Plato's philosophy, also wish to create a harmonious society through a drastic change in people's diet and temperament. Their vision is of a global transition to a "plant-based diet," in order to reduce agricultural emissions in line with current climate-change goals, and to provide enough food to meet the needs of a massively expanded global population by 2050. This will be part of an even more fundamental transformation that will make the world a fairer, more equitable place, as we give up—individually and as nations—a wide variety of selfish, harmful behaviors. This transformation may eventually include the abandonment of nations themselves. In recent years, this has come to be called "the Great Reset," including by its globalist architects, who also coined the facile slogan "Build Back Better" to describe it.

Unfortunately, the Great Reset is a topic that invites wild speculation about secret bloodlines, long-cherished eugenic dreams, and what Bill Gates really gets up to in his spare time when he takes off that awful lilac sweater—all of which makes it hard for us to talk about this anything but hidden program without being labeled a "conspiracy theorist."

I just want to deal with the facts, as I did in *The Eggs Benedict Option*. I'm not interested in the founder of the World Economic Forum, Klaus Schwab, and whether or not his father was a committed Nazi and how that might have influenced his son's dreams for world domination. The World Economic Forum is not a secret government, and Klaus Schwab is not really pulling the strings. What matters, rather, is the fact that the powers-that-be—governments, NGOs, corporations, the scientific establishment, media and powerful celebrities—are all lining up behind the Great Reset and telling us the world is going to change beyond recognition in the coming decades. We should take them at their word. They think their plan is great.

The Planetary Health Diet is the most comprehensive vision of a global plant-based diet we've seen so far, and it has the backing of the World Economic Forum, the UN, corporations and the scientific establishment.[137] The Diet is a product of the EAT-Lancet Commission on Food, Planet, Health, a collaboration between the EAT Foundation, a Norwegian philanthropic organisation, and the Lancet, the prestigious medical journal. The Diet provides a detailed model of exactly what the average global citizen of 2050 could be eating, providing a calorie breakdown by macro-nutrient and food types.

The Commission proceeded from two assumptions: First, that by 2050 the world will have a population of ten billion people, all of whom will need not just to be fed but fed a healthy diet; and second, that this must be done in a way that allows the UN's Sustainable Development Goals and the Paris Agreement on climate change to be respected. The Commission also assumed, "Healthy diets have an optimal calorie intake and consist largely of a diversity of plant-based foods, low amounts of animal source foods, contain unsaturated rather than saturated fats, and limited amounts of refined grain, highly processed foods and added sugars."[138]

The report gives an example diet for a calorie intake of 2,500 calories a day. The most important food group by calories is whole grains (811 calories), followed by unsaturated plant oils (354 calories), then nuts (291 calories), and legumes (284 calories). Fruits, dairy foods, and added sugars are each allocated somewhere around 100 calories a day. The smallest daily intakes are reserved for chicken and other poultry (62 calories), fish (40 calories), starchy vegetables (39 calories), beef, lamb, and pork (30 calories), and eggs (19 calories). Pictured as a plate divided among these foodstuffs by volume—not calories—half of the plate is covered by fruit and vegetables, and then two-thirds of the other half is taken up by whole grains, plant-sourced protein and unsaturated plant oils, with the remaining sixth taken up by starchy vegetables, dairy foods, animal protein, and added sugars.

If these numbers and ratios are hard to comprehend, consider the following examples. A typical egg will contain about 80 calories, so the Planetary Health Diet would allow you a quarter of an egg a day. Thirty calories a day from meat would be about 15 grams, give or take. That's a single slice from a packet of ham. A hundred calories from dairy would be less than 150ml of whole milk—a small glass—or 25g of cheddar cheese, which is a single normal slice.

So that's the nutrition side. It's left to organizations like the World Economic Forum to spell out the broader implications of a transition to a global plant-based diet, and in particular the fact it will rely on new forms of genetic modification to produce the grains and crops needed, and that this, together with the reliance on novel or "alternative" proteins like "plant-based meat" and lab-grown meat, means that corporate food producers will stand to benefit the most from the transition. It won't be small farmers or producers. In fact, they may no longer even exist.

This is illustrated in a detailed op-ed written by Civil Eats in 2021, which shows the degree to which the biggest food corporations in the world are already dominating the market for these so-called foods of the future.[139] Having captured a near monopoly on meat and dairy especially in the U.S., companies like Tyson and Cargill are now positioning themselves to break into new "ownership envelopes," including "plant-based meat," lab-grown meat, pea protein, aquaculture and insect protein. In doing so, they are reconfiguring and rebranding themselves, with a focus on particular macronutrients, and especially protein, rather than traditional foodstuffs. Tyson has already trademarked the slogan, "The Protein Company."

Corporations like to expand into new markets, of course, but what they also like is the degree of control these new commodities offer in the form of patents. Genetic modification and proprietary industrial processes mean that a product like "plant-based meat" or lab-grown meat can be owned in a way that a traditional animal product (like a steak) can't. This is what is really driving corporate expansion into plant-based foods and alternative proteins, not concern for health or the future of the planet.

Total corporate control is the real future of food—and we're well along that path already.

Corporate Control: A Disaster for Human Health

THE STORY of nutrition over the last 100 to 150 years is one of the growth of corporate control at the expense of human health, and the Great Reset will be a continuation, or perhaps the final act, of this story. Put simply, corporations have taken control of the food supply to an ever-greater extent, and our health has deteriorated to a corresponding degree. There's no better index of corporate control of the food supply today than the amount of processed food people consume.

Processed food is also referred to as "ultra-processed food" to distinguish healthy, time-honored forms like cheese and properly fermented bread from Twinkies, Cheetos, and microwaveable meals. Food has been processed since the dawn of human history, since the first half-ape dropped a slab of meat on a fire and then ate the cooked product. While there's some wrangling over the definitions of "processed" and "ultra-processed food"—especially from researchers funded by the food conglomerates who want to trash the notion that ultra-processed food has negative effects—a decent working definition of "ultra-processed food" would be something like, "food that is produced in a factory, contains ingredients that would not typically be found in a home kitchen, and is sold to consumers in special packaging, usually plastic." That definition covers pretty much all the most harmful foodstuffs that the modern industrial food system is producing and that people (especially the younger generations) are pouring down their throats more and more each day.

Toddlers in the UK—children aged between two and five—now get 61 percent of their daily calories from ultra-processed food.[140] Adolescents in the UK, aged 11–18, derive an even larger proportion of their daily calories from ultra-processed food: 65.9 percent according to a recently published study.[141] This is simply an unprecedented situation in human history—these products didn't exist until the last century—and it bodes very badly for the future. Consumption will increase. It may not reach 100 percent for the general population, but there already are and there will be more people who derive their entire "nutrition" from food that is made in a factory and sold to them on a supermarket shelf, wrapped in plastic.

The Price of Degeneration

THE PROCESS of supplanting natural whole foods with processed foods in the West began at least a century ago, and its negative effects were immediately visible. This is the real theme of what I consider to be the greatest book on nutrition ever written, Weston A. Price's 1939 book *Nutrition and Physical Degeneration*. Price became a dentist in Cleveland, Ohio, at the turn of the 20th century, a time when even rural Americans were starting to move away from what we might call their traditional diets, based on simply prepared, locally produced whole foods, to a diet of foods produced in factories. Price noticed a curious phenomenon among his patients, a literal process of physical degeneration, mainly in the children. Not only were more and more of his patients coming to him with mouths riddled with cavities, but the entire structure of their faces was collapsing, or not forming properly in the first place. They had crowded teeth, poorly formed dental arches—that's the roof of the mouth—as well as narrow cheeks and nostrils and recessed jaws. These physical changes were accompanied by behavioral changes and learning difficulties that had been almost totally unknown before.

Price rightly surmised that changing diet was the cause, but he wanted to be scientific. To do that, he needed to establish a control for comparison, which meant looking in detail at groups that were not consuming new industrial diets but still eating the foods their ancestors ate. Price finally got the chance to do this in the early 1930s, and so began a globe-trotting adventure with his wife that took them to traditional small-scale societies on almost every inhabited continent. The Prices went from the Arctic Circle to Africa, from the Scottish Highlands and Islands to the Islands of the South Pacific, to the Torres Strait, Fiji, and New Zealand.

Wherever the Prices encountered peoples who still followed their ancestral diets, there they found "physically perfect people," in Weston Price's own words. These people not only displayed beautiful facial structure and development, but they were well grown, physically strong, and displayed remarkable resilience and resistance to disease, too. One of the great contributions of the book was to establish that oral and facial health is a primary index of health more broadly. This is something modern medicine is only beginning, dimly, to understand. A recent study showed, for example, that bad oral hygiene is directly associated with the formation of plaques in the brain associated with Alzheimer's disease. Pathogenic bacteria multiply in the mouth and make their way to the brain, where they cause changes to brain cells that protect against degenerative diseases.[142] You can't be healthy if you have an unhealthy mouth.

Although Weston Price found variation across diets—as we might expect if we were to compare people whose main occupation is hunting seals and caribou in the Arctic with crofters and fishermen on a Scottish island or pastoralists herding cattle by the River Nile—there was still a significant continuity. Every single one of the dozen or so "physically perfect peoples" he found built their diet on consumption of nutrient-dense animal foods: organ meat, blood products, fatty cuts of meat, eggs, shellfish, and dairy.

Here's Price's description of the people of the high Alpine Loetschental Valley in Switzerland, who lived on a diet of rye bread, raw dairy products—milk, cheese and butter—some meat, and the occasional fish from a mountain brook—all of which came from their immediate surroundings:

> The people of the Loetschental Valley make up a community of two thousand who have been a world unto themselves. They have neither physician nor dentist because they have so little need for them; they have neither policeman nor jail, because they have no need for them. The clothing has been the substantial homespuns made from the wool of their

sheep. The valley has produced not only everything that is needed for clothing, but practically everything that is needed for food. It has been the achievement of the valley to build some of the finest physiques in all Europe. This is attested by the fact that many of the famous Swiss Guards of the Vatican, who are the admiration of the world and are the pride of Switzerland, have been selected from this and other Alpine valleys. It is every Loetschental boy's ambition to be a Vatican guard. Notwithstanding the fact that tuberculosis is the most serious disease of Switzerland, according to a statement given me by a government official, a recent report of this valley did not reveal a single case.[143]

Price described the Maori of New Zealand, who ate "very liberally" from the sea and prized certain highly nutritious shellfish, especially during pregnancy, as standing "on the pedestal of perfection" for their "splendid physiques." He notes how he examined a "young Maori man who stands about six feet four inches and weighs 230 pounds":

The Maori race developed a knowledge of Nature's laws and adopted a system of living in harmony with those laws to so high a degree that they were able to build what was reported by early scientists to be the most physically perfect race living on the face of the earth. They accomplished this largely through diet and a system of social organization designed to provide a high degree of perfection in their offspring. To do this, they utilized foods from the sea very liberally. The fact that they were able to maintain an immunity from dental caries [cavities] so high that only one tooth in two thousand had been attacked by tooth decay (which is probably as high a degree of immunity as that of any contemporary race) is a strong argument in favor od their plan of life.[144]

These groups in perfect physical health understood the crucial value of the nutrient-dense animal foods they consumed. Often, their consumption of these foods would be surrounded by ceremonies and even taboos, like the following practice of the Nuer, a pastoralist group from the south of Sudan. The Nuer believed that a "man's character and physical growth depend upon how well he feeds [his] soul by eating the livers of animals":

> The liver is so sacred that it may not be touched by human hands. It is accordingly always handled with their spear or saber, or with specially prepared forked sticks. It is eaten both raw and cooked.[145]

And although these groups did consume plant foods regularly—grains were consumed by the Loetschental Swiss and Highland Scots, for example, and certain plants like the water hyacinth were important for Nile tribes to prevent goiters from lack of iodine—Price was absolutely clear that optimal health cannot be built on a plant-based diet, or even a diet that leans most heavily on plants with small amounts of animal foods. "It is significant," he says, "that I have as yet found no group that was building and maintaining good bodies exclusively on plant foods. A number of groups are endeavoring to do so with marked evidence of failure."[146]

Price's Warning

PROBLEMS FOR these traditional groups coincided with the spread of what Weston Price called "the displacing foods of our modern civilization," foodstuffs produced in factories—canned goods, refined-wheat products—that were the early precursors of the ultra-processed food we eat today in such prodigious amounts. Wherever the natives stopped eating nutrient-dense animal foods and started eating like modern Westerners, the same profound physical changes arose that Price saw back in Cleveland, Ohio: the same tooth decay, the same malformation of the mouth, cheeks, nose and jaw—the entire face—and other broader changes, including increased susceptibility to disease and shortened stature. Price collected data that showed the inhabitants of the Scottish Highlands, previously among the tallest people in Europe, had shrunk significantly in recent decades as they moved away from their traditional diet of meat, dairy products, and oats:

> On my return from the Outer Hebrides to Scotland, I was concerned to obtain information from government officials relative to the incidence of tooth decay and the degenerative diseases in various parts of north Scotland. I was advised that in the last fifty years the average height of Scotch men in some parts decreased four inches, and that this had been coincident with the general change from high immunity to dental caries to a loss of immunity in a great part of this general district. A study of the market places revealed that a large part of the nutrition was shipped into the district in the form of refined flours and canned goods and sugar. There were very few herds of dairy cattle to be seen. It was explained that even the highland cattle did not do as well as formerly on the same ranges.[147]

Probably the most striking aspect of *Nutrition and Physical Degeneration*, which makes its thesis about the abandonment of traditional diets even harder to resist, is the series of portraits of identical twins Weston Price photographed with his camera. In many different locations, Price was able to find twins who had taken opposing paths in terms of their diet. One had stuck with the traditional foods and the other had opted, for whatever reason, for the "displacing foods of our modern civilization." Without exception, the twins who had stuck to the foods of their ancestors displayed perfect physical development, while their brothers and sisters were plagued with the tell-tale signs of physical degeneration. The contrast between the two sets of twins, placed side by side on the page, could hardly be greater.

We can already say with certainty what the health effects of a transition to a global plant-based diet will be. While getting everybody to abandon meat and dairy products *might* "save the planet" from climate change, and while it *might* feed a world of 10 billion people, it *will* be a disaster for human health, especially men's health, as well as severely reducing our freedom of choice and action. (Note the *mights* there: there are very strong reasons to doubt all of the claims made by advocates of plant-based diets, not just the health claims, but also the claims about the environmental and humanitarian impact of abandoning animal agriculture as we know it.)

A Plant-Based Disaster

PLANT-BASED DIETS are maladaptive for a number of reasons. I could tell you simply to look at a few vegetarians and vegans, or to look up a few of the horror stories about babies and children fed vegan diets, but I'll play the ball and not the man. Let's consider, in basic terms, the main reasons why vegetarian and vegan diets are inferior to diets rich in animal foods. These fall into four categories: protein quality, nutrient density (including vitamin and mineral content), fat types, and phytoestrogens.

With regard to protein quality, plant proteins are less complete than animal proteins, meaning they contain fewer of the essential amino acids (the building blocks for proteins) and lack some of them entirely, and we have a harder time absorbing protein from plants. Of course, food labelling doesn't tell you this—that the 20g of protein you're supposed to be getting from a serving of soy or beans is significantly less useful than the equivalent 20g you'd get

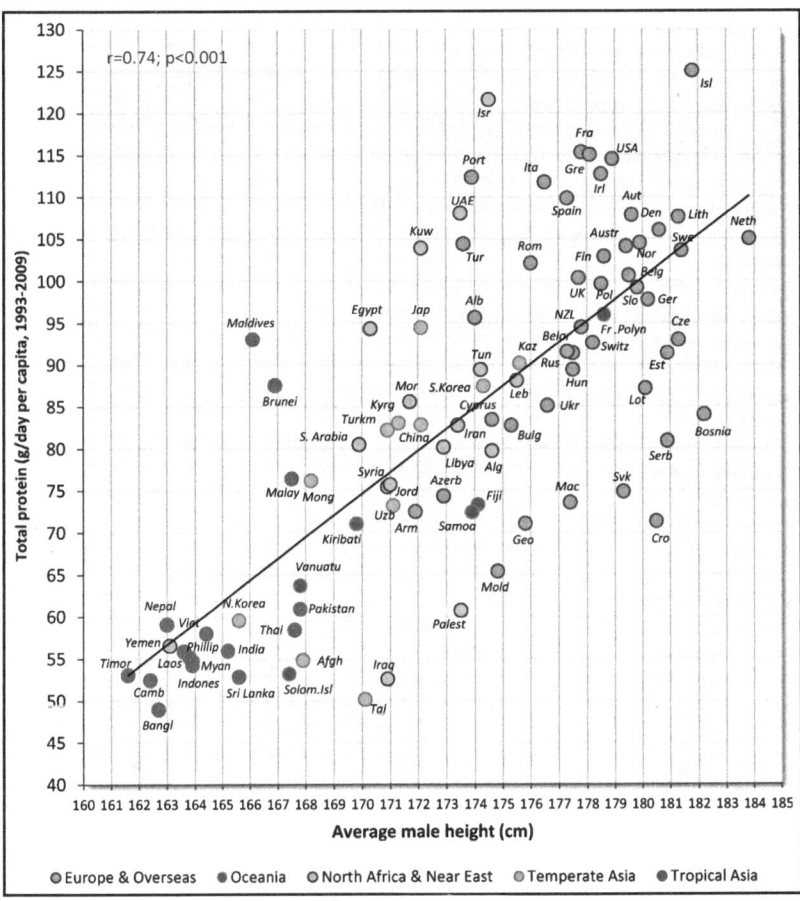

CORRELATION BETWEEN MALE HEIGHT IN 93 COUNTRIES AND THE AVERAGE DAILY CONSUMPTION OF TOTAL PROTEIN (FAOSTAT, 1993–2009), P. GRASGRUBER ET AL. / ECONOMICS AND HUMAN BIOLOGY 21 (2016)[148]

from a serving of steak or milk—but it's true. A meta-analysis of sixteen studies on the relative benefits of animal versus plant proteins for building muscle spells this out clearly: "animal protein tends to have a more favorable effect on lean mass compared to plant protein, and the benefit appears more pronounced in younger adults."[149]

The superiority of animal protein is also demonstrated by another study that showed a significant global relationship between height and protein sources. Researchers took anthropometric and food-consumption data from 105 countries around the world, and divided countries into three groups based on the main sources of protein in their diet: rice-based, wheat-based and milk-based. The researchers showed that rice-based diets, associated with tropical Asia, produce the shortest people, followed by wheat-based diets, which are associated with the Middle East and North Africa. Milk-based diets, typical of northern and central Europe, produce the tallest people in the world. The researchers conclude, "[Plant-based diets] are not able to provide the optimal stimuli for physical growth, even if the intake of total protein and total energy poses no problem. In fact, we observed a difference of 10 cm (174 cm vs. 184 cm) between nations relying on the surplus of plant and animal proteins, respectively."[150]

When I say that plant-based diets are less nutrient-dense, I mean that they lack compounds that are essential for human health. There are of course plant compounds that can't be found in animal foods, but the truth is, these are far less important for us than the compounds plants lack. B vitamins are almost totally missing in plant foods, especially vitamin B12. A B12 deficiency can be devastating. It can cause, among other things, infertility, mental illness, and various forms of neurological damage. Many vegetarians and vegans supplement with B12 for as long as they stick to their diets, but a significant proportion don't because they're simply unaware of what they're missing. Sixty percent of adult vegans are estimated to have a B12 deficiency, and 40 percent of adult vegetarians.[151] Vitamin D3, which is involved in calcium absorption and bone health, is another essential vitamin vegetarians and vegans are generally deficient in. Vegans have been shown to have fracture rates that are 30 percent higher than those of meat-eaters.[152]

I could continue. Iron, zinc, glycine, iodine, creatine, choline, selenium, methionine and taurine—vegans are likely to be deficient in one or more or all of these things as well.

And cholesterol. Vegetarian and vegan diets are severely lacking (or even absent) in cholesterol, which is one of the main reasons why they're recommended as being healthy. Eating cholesterol (and saturated fat) raises blood cholesterol, which causes heart disease, which causes death, or so the theory, often referred to as the "lipid-heart hypothesis," has it. Lierre Keith, author of *The Vegetarian Myth*, describes this as "the bulwark that the nutritional vegetarians will stand behind." By "nutritional vegetarians," she means those who advocate vegetarian diets on nutritional as opposed to ethical grounds, although it's possible to do both, of course.

I could write an entire book on the topic of the "lipid-heart hypothesis," why it's wrong and always was wrong and, just as importantly, why it came to be accepted despite the scientific establishment at the time knowing that it was obviously wrong and that the man promoting it, a self-proclaimed nutritionist called Ancel Keys, was a fraud whose only qualification for calling himself such was helping to design the K-Ration during World War II. Thankfully someone else already has written this book: Dr.

Malcolm Kendrick. In *The Great Cholesterol Con*,[153] Kendrick details the abject failure of the lipid-heart hypothesis. Catherine Shanahan also addresses this topic in her popular book *Deep Nutrition*,[154] which I also recommend.

You Need Cholesterol

YOUR DOCTOR will probably still tell you, once he or she has calmed down, to stop consuming 12 eggs and three portions of steak cooked in butter a day. Food advertising for products like margarine or "plant-based eggs" will still tout the lack of cholesterol as a health benefit. But the lipid-hypothesis has now been pretty much overturned. The evidence that consuming dietary cholesterol raises blood cholesterol, and that having higher blood cholesterol is bad for you, has been largely if not totally discredited. In 2015, most notably, the USDA quietly dropped its recommendation for dietary cholesterol intake, years after health authorities in other nations had done so.[155] Cholesterol is no longer a "nutrient of concern."

Cholesterol should never have been a "nutrient of concern." I've already discussed the molecule's vital role in the production of sex hormones, which are essential for human health, but it's not an exaggeration to say that without cholesterol, human life would be impossible. As Lierre Keith puts it, humans would be "puddles" without cholesterol because it's what makes our cell membranes impermeable to water. No cholesterol, no cell membranes; no cell membranes, no body. Cholesterol is also essential to the function of the nervous system, whose synapses are made almost entirely of cholesterol, and well over 20 percent of the body's cholesterol is in the brain, which is made up of 60 percent saturated fat.

In truth, we should never have demonized cholesterol in the first place. Doing so has damaged the health of, and probably killed, many thousands, maybe millions of people. Low blood cholesterol, far from being health-preserving, is a killer. In the Minnesota Coronary Experiment, a double-blind randomized controlled trial, patients at seven institutions in Minnesota were given vegetable oil instead of saturated fats, with the aim of reducing their cholesterol and helping them live longer. The opposite happened. For every 30-point decrease in cholesterol observed, the death rate increased by 22 percent.[156] The results were suppressed for decades because they totally upended the false orthodoxy about cholesterol. These aren't isolated findings either. A Finnish study of over-75s found that individuals with cholesterol levels in the highest third had death rates that were half those of individuals with the lowest.[157] A massive study of nearly 13 million Korean adults showed that low total cholesterol was associated with increased risk of all-cause mortality—if you have low cholesterol, you're more likely to die of just about anything.[158] And a study of 6,000 French men also showed a clear link between low cholesterol and mortality. Men with lower cholesterol had a significantly increased risk of dying from cancer over a seventeen-year period.[159]

The kind of fats vegetarians and vegans consume instead of animal fats—seed and vegetable oils—are a novelty in human history, having only been consumed in any quantity by humans in the last century or so. If you've seen the memes—and I'm assuming that if you've been hanging around Twitter at all, you have—you'll know these oils were once considered fit only to be used as paint thinners and engine lubricants. Would that they were still so! Because it isn't only vegetarians and vegans who consume them. We all do, in massive quantities, especially through processed food, which is loaded with the stuff.

Seed Oils and Chronic Disease

IT'S NOT just because they don't contain cholesterol that seed and vegetable oils are bad. It's also because these oils are inherently reactive, because of the types of fat (polyunsaturated fats) they contain, which are less chemically stable than the saturated fats that predominate in animal foods. Polyunsaturated fats form reactive species in the body that attack the tissues, causing damage and inflammation, which is the starting point for virtually all chronic diseases. It's no surprise, then, to discover that pretty much all the prevailing diseases of modernity, from heart disease to cancer, are starting to be linked to consumption of polyunsaturated fats. Studies also show that the type of fatty acids most commonly found in seed and vegetable oils, especially omega-6 fatty acids, are associated with weight gain. Omega 6s have been found to stimulate the body's endocannabinoid system, which is responsible for appetite regulation. Mice consistently gain more weight the more linoleic acid, an omega-6 fatty acid, they are fed.[160]

Consider soybean oil, for example, consumption of which has increased a thousandfold over the last century. A study from 2020 showed that as well as being obesogenic, soybean oil causes serious genetic dysregulation and neurological damage in mice.[161] The genes affected included genes associated with inflammation, neuroendocrine and neurochemical processes, insulin signaling, and the production of oxytocin, the "love hormone," which is responsible for social bonding, among other things. Other genes that were affected are linked to neurological diseases, including Alzheimer's disease, Parkinson's, and autism. The authors of the study conclude that, although the study was conducted on mice, the results are likely to hold for humans as well: "the [soybean-oil-rich] American diet may be not only contributing to increased rates of metabolic disease but also affecting neurological function."[162]

Plants and Phytoestrogens

FINALLY, LET'S briefly look at phytoestrogens: plant compounds that have estrogenic effects. These compounds work in more or less the same manner as the harmful industrial compounds I described earlier in the book. Certain plants have been used for centuries in traditional medicine as treatments for women's problems including menopausal symptoms because of their estrogenic properties, or, as I noted earlier, as a way for men, especially religious devotees, to suppress their masculine urges.

Soy receives particular attention for good reason. It's held up as a "superfood" and one of the best plant sources of protein. Soy and other legumes are central to today's vegetarian and vegan diets, and they are intended to be even more so in the global plant-based diet of the future. Although soy has been consumed for centuries in Asia, it has never been consumed in large quantity on a daily basis—i.e. as a major protein source—and it was consumed in fermented forms that bear little resemblance to the soy people consume now when they eat a plant-based burger or chug a Soylent meal-replacement drink. Fermentation is an important traditional food-preparation technique that has fallen by the wayside in the modern era; although it's started making a pretty big comeback in recent years as improving gut health has become a mainstream trend.

Fermenting soy deactivates the phytoestrogens, particularly the isoflavones, that are responsible for soy's feminizing effects. Fermentation also disables the trypsin inhibitors in soy, which prevent protein digestion and cause bloating and wind when people consume it unfermented.

Scientific research into the effects of soy has become heavily politicized in recent years, mainly because of the so-called "soyboy conspiracy theory," but also because soy is huge business.[163] Soy is the second most important crop in the U.S., second only to corn, so it's not a surprise to find a robust response from the scientific community against claims that soy consumption is harmful for humans.

The animal studies, certainly, are unequivocal. I talked earlier about perhaps my favorite scientific study of all time, the one that shows how soy turns male macaques into passive-aggressive incel-monkeys, but that's just one of a huge number of studies that reveal the gender-bending effects of soy on a variety of different animals, from monkeys to rodents. On the basis of these studies, we have every reason to believe that soy could have similar or even the same effects on humans. But things are complicated by the existence of a significant number of badly designed and misleading human studies. One of the main problems with the human studies is that they're deceptively framed. The vast majority don't consider soy consumption in the long term. They look at short periods of consumption, usually less than 90 days, and then conclude that there are no negative hormonal effects for either sex but especially for men.[164]

When we look at anecdotal studies of longer-term consumption, we start to see things like erectile dysfunction, loss of libido and, of course, man boobs. Take this case study, for example.[165] A 54-year-old man presented himself to doctors with erectile dysfunction and gynecomastia. Blood tests showed that the man had low testosterone and a hormonal profile indicative of hypogonadism (reduced function of the testicles), but he had no history of the condition. The cause of his problems remained unclear until he told the doctors that he had been consuming over a liter of soy milk a day for the last three years. When he gave up the soy milk, his symptoms improved significantly within eight weeks.

We've Been Here Before

THE ADOPTION of uniform vegetarianism (or even veganism) will be the culmination of a long process of abandoning traditional whole foods, and especially animal foods, that has taken place over the last 150 years and seen control of the food supply transferred into the hands of a smaller and smaller number of mega corporations. With the creation of novel ingredients like seed and vegetable oils and the class of industrially produced food known as "processed" or "ultra-processed" food, we were promised renewed health as well as convenience. Instead, we have been sapped of our vitality like never before and made subject to new forms of domination by big food, big pharma and big government. For the social planners, on the other hand, a further decline in *thymos* and our individual and collective scope for political action may be no bad thing—far from it.

We've been here before. Human civilization has already been radically changed through a change to the way food is produced and controlled. That's precisely what the Agricultural Revolution, often referred to as the Neolithic Revolution, was: a total transformation of Stone Age society that took place because of a shift from subsistence hunter-gathering, and maybe some very primitive exercises in early farming, to fixed-field farming and the rearing of a small number of domesticated animals. The Agricultural Revolution took place about 10,000–12,000 years ago in the Near East, in an area between the Tigris and Euphrates rivers that's often referred to as the "Southern Alluvium" because its bountiful soils were fed by the deposition of silt and clay—alluvium—from those two mighty rivers. It was there that conditions were right, it seems, for an experiment in food production that would change the course of human history forever.

In *The Eggs Benedict Option*, I called the Agricultural Revolution the "Original Great Reset." Here's how the man who created the term "Great Reset," Richard Florida, defines it:

> Great Resets are broad and fundamental transformations of the economic and social order and involve much more than strictly economic or financial events. A true Reset transforms not simply the way we innovate and produce but also ushers in a whole new economic landscape . . . Eventually, it ushers in a whole new way of life—defined by new wants and needs and new models of consumption that spur the economy, enabling industry to expand and productivity to improve, while creating new jobs for workers.[166]

Florida had more recent events in mind, like the "economic resets" of America in the 1870s and the Great Depression, but there's no reason his term can't be applied to a much more distant event. Everything Florida includes in his definition applies to the Agricultural Revolution and its effects, which made urban civilization as we know it possible. Within a relatively short period of time, man went from living in small roving bands of hunter-gatherers, probably numbering no more than a few hundred, to inhabiting early city states like Ur and Uruk, unheralded conglomerations of people—maybe as many as 50,000—that were surrounded by walls and had their own militaries, bureaucracies, and merchant and slave classes.

The First Great Reset and the Damage Done

THE AGRICULTURAL Revolution is usually presented as a triumphalist narrative. We are, after all, children of that transition, and many of the things we most value about ourselves and our modern societies are a direct or indirect result of man's abandonment of the hunter-gatherer life. But recent scholarship, including the synthesis of the late anthropologist James C. Scott, tells a different story.[167] The Agricultural Revolution was as much a process of human domestication as of plant and animal domestication. At every turn it was resisted, with good reason, by the earliest farmers, who (the evidence suggests) were probably forced to farm by predatory outsiders who became the new elites of the first grain states. Only a "gun to the head" theory—perhaps a combination of ecological change in the Near East and human conflict, with the capture of slaves as its central goal—can fully explain why the Agricultural Revolution took place and wasn't later abandoned.

"Domestication was not a one-way street," I note in *The Eggs Benedict Option*.[168] By that I mean that man domesticated animals and plants, but by doing so also domesticated and changed himself. We can consistently identify early agriculturalists from their skeletons alone, in the same way we can distinguish wild boars from pigs and aurochs from cows. Domesticated humans bear a distinctive physical syndrome that marks them out from their hunter-gatherer peers and ancestors. The bones of the women, for example, have bent-under toes and deformed knees from all the time

147

they spent grinding grains on the floor with stones. More broadly, we see physical shrinkage and unmistakable evidence of nutritional deficiencies, stress, and disease. Experts note that nutritional deficiencies are not widely observed until the advent of grain agriculture. Rickets, anemia and tooth decay become particularly evident as a result of the early farmers' diet, rich in carbohydrates but lacking in protein and fat. Evidence of soft-tissue conditions is harder to find, obviously—little to no soft tissue remains after all this time—but there is some written evidence that suggests beri-beri, pellagra, riboflavin deficiency, and kwashiorkor would have been common, as we'd expect from modern cases of chronic malnutrition.

Nutritional deficiencies in particular would have put the early farmers at greater risk from new infectious diseases that developed as a result of the totally novel concentrations of people and animals brought together by the Agricultural Revolution. James C. Scott has called the new settlements "feedlots" for pathogens, with good reason. Pretty much all of the major infectious diseases that are specifically adapted for humans arrived in the last ten thousand years, many of them in the last five thousand. Since their arrival these diseases have represented the major share of all human mortality.

Pioneering new genetic analysis is also suggesting clear behavioral changes, not just for diet (e.g. changes to metabolism to adjust to a largely grain-based diet) but also for social behavior. We know that domesticated animals experience profound changes to emotional reactivity via changes to the brain's limbic system, which governs fear, aggression and threat response. There's reason to believe such changes were mirrored, at least to some extent, in humans adapting to their altered existence in the first agricultural settlements. A scientific study from 2022, "Population Genomics of Stone Age Eurasia," identifies a number of telling genetic variants in early farmer populations. Genes "associated with mood-related disorders, like increased anxiety, guilty feelings, and irritability are over-represented in Anatolian farmer ancestry."[169] Further research will no doubt reveal other genetic and behavioral changes associated with the Agricultural Revolution.

The domestication analogy can be pushed even further if we consider that many of the early agriculturalists were *slaves*, and that slaves were generally considered to be nothing more than domesticated animals, not fully human. Aristotle meant it when he said that slaves are tools of the household just like oxen. Coercion was probably necessary to create the early agricultural states in the first place, but it was also essential to keep the "population machines" of these early states in motion. Cities like Ur and Uruk were incredibly fragile, and liable to collapse at any moment, because the death rate from infectious diseases was probably so high and because ordinary people were looking to escape at any opportunity. Most early warfare wasn't about taking territory or killing so much as capturing people, with a preference for potential workers but also reproductive-age women. Constant influxes of captured women may have been the only way to maintain a stable birth rate.

James C. Scott describes a "Golden Age of Barbarians," which lasted until the modern era, so perhaps around the 17th or 18th century AD, when it was still possible to escape life as an agriculturalist and "go over to the barbarians."[170] Throughout this period there was still territory the modern state didn't dominate, which meant a different way of life was possible. Scott calls this choice to lay down tools and make a new life "voluntary self-nomadization." Herodotus, for example, described how certain Greeks would spend part of the year in the saddle with the nomadic Scythians, but other peoples, especially peasants, would make the change for good. It's part of the reason states and city-states built walls: they wanted to keep enemies out, sure, but they also wanted to keep their own populations *in*. The Great Wall kept the Xiong-nu and the Mongols and the Manchu at bay—some of the time—but it also made it much harder for belabored Chinese cultivators to reach the endless grasslands of the Eurasian steppe—and freedom.

The collapse of early states may look to us through the long telescope of time like little "dark ages," when written and other physical evidence disappears from the record, and we just assume that things got very bad for the former inhabitants of those states, but the opposite is just as likely to be true.

There may well be, then, a great deal to be said on behalf of classical dark ages in terms of human well-being. Much of the dispersion that characterizes them is likely to be a flight from war, taxes, epidemics, crop failures and conscription. As such, it may staunch the worst losses that arise from concentrated sedentism under state rule.[171]

Resisting the Plant-Based Future

THE SPREAD of new industrially produced foodstuffs, both within the Western world and beyond it, to places like Fiji and even the Arctic, was a disaster for human health, from the very beginning. The 20th century saw as profound a shift in human diet as took place during the Agricultural Revolution in the Near East, 10,000–12,000 years ago. The displacing foods Weston Price identified as being responsible for physical degeneration have themselves been displaced by newer generations of processed or ultra-processed foods, and the physical degeneration has deepened. This transformation has been driven by corporate food producers, who have gained control of the food supply to an ever-greater extent, making it harder and harder for people to eat in the manner of their ancestors. Now, with today's plant-based agenda and the climate crisis, corporate food producers can go even further and stake a claim to a global food supply they can own through patents down to the genetic level. Just like the early agriculturalists of the Near East, corralled into the first cities and forced to subsist on a meager diet of grains, we will be cut off from the life-giving nutrient-dense animal foods that are necessary for optimal development and health.

Just like the inhabitants of Plato's "community of pigs," our *thymos* will be sapped even further. We may have "harmony," but at what cost?

It's possible, of course, to revolt against this situation. At the recent Paris Olympics, which were heralded as the first "vegan" or "plant-based" games, many of the national teams refused to forego animal products. Organizers had included stipulations that a majority of the food on offer for athletes in the Olympic Village should be vegan to reduce the carbon footprint of the competition. So what happened? Teams like the Australians just shipped in their own meat, eggs, and dairy instead, at their own cost. "More than 700kg of eggs and a tonne of extra meat has been ordered to replace fake meat meals and non-dairy options," reported *The Australian.*[172]

This was deeply embarrassing for the organizers and for the propagandists of plant-based diets, who wanted to be able to say that optimal athletic performance is possible on a vegetarian or vegan diet. Such claims have been a key part of the push behind plant-based diets, and we've seen opportunists like Arnold Schwarzenegger, who consumed ungodly quantities of steak, raw eggs, and raw milk during his bodybuilding career, give their support to high-profile media on the subject, including the 2018 documentary *The Game Changers*. Instead, the athletes at Paris 2024 showed the world what it already knew, or should have known. Plant-based diets simply can't compete with the foods our ancestors ate for hundreds of thousands, even millions, of years before some of us decided things had to change. When the story broke last year, I tried to tell people to make the most of it and even wrote articles about it, but much less was made of this stunning defeat than could have been. In large part, this is simply a reflection of the media's role as propagandists for the plant-based agenda.

Symbolic victories won't be enough. Nor will market forces. It's already abundantly clear that given a free choice, ordinary people don't want to give up meat and animal products. The ongoing woes of alternative-protein "big beasts" like Impossible Burger and Beyond Meat, which are hemorrhaging staff and profits, show this. In 2021, over 70 percent of Australian men who took part in a survey said they'd rather lose ten years of their life than give up meat.[173] Veganism may be on the rise, but it still represents a tiny fraction of the population. Just over 3 percent of Europeans in 2023, according to research.[174]

Manufacturers of plant-based alternatives have already started to shift their advertising to recognize that consumers know their products don't taste better and aren't better for you than the real animal products they're intended to replace. Oatly, the "oat milk" brand, is a great example. As part of its "Help Dad" campaign, Oatly ran a series of ads in which woke teenagers ambush their bewildered fathers at the refrigerator and shame them for daring to want a glass of cow's milk. This strategy, relying on social pressure, has the backing of detailed consumer research. One study, published in late 2021, reports that meat-eaters are more likely to choose vegetarian options in a restaurant if at least 75 percent of the menu options are vegetarian.[175] Another shows that battering consumers with the "social and health costs" of eating meat compared to plant-based foods is by far the best way to get them to drop meat and dairy and eat new plant-based alternatives instead.[176] The message is clear: make people feel guilty and don't give them a choice.

Removing consumer choice from the equation—real consumer choice—is the best way to understand what's going on with plant-based foods and alternative proteins. Despite the high-profile failures of companies like Beyond Meat and Impossible, billions of dollars are still pouring into startups focusing on "alternative proteins" and "foods of the future," and food giants like Tyson are still reconfiguring their operations and rebranding away from traditional foodstuffs like meat to macronutrients, mainly protein. These companies expect a significant change in consumer behavior, but one that's not driven by consumers themselves, and they expect it soon. These companies are banking on a near-future where, through a combination of inflation, artificial scarcity, and punitive taxes on products that are supposedly most harmful for the environment, ordinary people simply won't be able to eat meat all that often, if ever. It's been my contention for some time now that no government is going to ban meat outright because that would be far too unpopular, and I stand by that. It would be much better, I think, to allow "objective forces" to stop people from eating meat and drinking milk, and allow declining consumption to be framed as a "necessary sacrifice" rather than making animal foods illegal.

A 2022 op-ed for *The New York Times*, written as food inflation and the effects of supply-chain disruption due to the pandemic were making life very hard for consumers, spells out the strategy. "You Want to Buy Meat? In this Economy?" was the title:

> Inflation has the potential to drive welcome change for the planet if Americans think differently about the way they eat. While hunger and food insecurity are a very real problem in the United States and globally, middle- and upper-class Americans still have more choices at the grocery store than perhaps any food shoppers in history. Climate change has motivated some to eat less resource-intensive meat and more vegetables, grains and legumes, but this movement has not reached the scale necessary to bring needed change—yet.[177]

Ominously, the author even praised the 1917 Lever Act, which allowed the U.S. government to requisition food from citizens and prevent hoarding. After events of the last four years, I wouldn't bet against anything, including meat confiscations. But I doubt it will come to that.

Animal-Based Food as a Basic Right

MY ARGUMENT in *The Eggs Benedict Option* is that the only way to fight the plant-based agenda is with a political movement that makes access to nutrient-dense animal foods a basic right and protects traditional agriculture. It could and should also promote better forms of agriculture, like regenerative farming as practiced by farmers like Joel Salatin, but at base it needs to guarantee the availability of animal foods as an essential need. There are stirrings of such a movement in the U.S. at least, but we need to go much farther, much quicker if we want to ensure meat and eggs and milk are still on the menu in the coming years.

In 2024, Ron DeSantis became the first U.S. governor to ban the production and sale of lab-grown meat within his state, making it a second-degree misdemeanour, with a prison sentence of up to 60 days. After signing the bill into law, DeSantis said that his aim was to protect Florida's "vibrant agricultural industry . . . against acts of man, against an ideological agenda that wants to finger agriculture as the problem, that views things like raising cattle as destroying our climate." He railed at the hypocrisy of the Davos class "who will lecture the rest of us about things like global warming. They will say that, you know, you can't drive an internal combustion engine vehicle, they'll say that agriculture is bad. Meanwhile, they're flying to Davos in their private jets."[178] "While the World Economic Forum is telling the world to forgo meat consumption, Florida is increasing meat production and encouraging residents to continue to consume and enjoy 100 percent real Florida beef," a press release from the governor's office said.[179]

As much as it might pain free-marketeers, this is a good start. The plant-based agenda has the backing of governments, NGOs, corporations, the media, and the scientific establishment. This alliance will not be beaten in farm shops and supermarkets. Consumer choice didn't save the earliest farmers from the horrors of the Agricultural Revolution. They, at least, could vote with their feet and run away when the opportunity presented itself—and they did. We, on the other hand, have nowhere to run. The plant-based agenda is a global one, and must be fought where we stand, in our communities and nations.

CHAPTER 6

What Can Be Done?

"An ounce of prevention is worth a pound of cure."

—BENJAMIN FRANKLIN

"The microplastics are already in our balls."

—MAC DAVIS, founder of Minicircle

— ✦✦✦ —

W E'VE SEEN the depth of the problem facing us, underlined most emphatically by the prediction that within just a few decades it could be impossible for us to reproduce as a species because of the speed and severity of the decline in sperm counts. The biological changes affecting men—and women—driven by exposure to endocrine-disrupting chemicals and our addiction to food that isn't really even food have taken on an existential character in a matter of a century or less. The first truly synthetic plastic, bakelite, was produced in 1907, but it wasn't until the middle of the century that our dependence on plastics really started to bite, and the same goes for processed food, which existed in its most primitive forms at the turn of the 20th century, but wasn't refined and developed into the forms we know and, unfortunately, love until decades later.

As we face this problem, it's easy to become thoroughly disillusioned, or "blackpilled," as the internet slang would have it. What's the point? How can we do anything about a problem on this scale?

I remember posting a study on Twitter about the feminizing effects of the air we breathe. My point was a basic one: When we're thinking about estrogenic chemicals, we tend to focus on chemicals that are ingested (food, water) or absorbed through the skin (personal-care products, etc.), and forget that inhalation is another important route for exposure. As a result of microplastic research there's been growing focus on inhalation, but it's still an underappreciated route for exposure. In the study in question, researchers in Italy took air samples from five different sites in rural and urban areas and assessed the particulate matter for cytotoxicity (cell-killing ability) and estrogenicity.[180] The researchers found that all of the samples contained cytotoxic and estrogenic compounds. Chemicals of note were benzo(a)pyrene and pesticides, bisphenol A, alkylphenols, polybrominated diphenyl ethers, polychlorinated biphenyls and polychlorinated dibenzodioxins or dibenzofurans. What was particularly surprising was that, although one of the rural areas had the lowest levels of cytotoxicity and estrogenicity, the other had levels that were higher than an urban incinerator site.

In conclusion, I jokingly suggested it might now be time for us all to start donning masks and embracing our inner Bane, the baddie from the Batman film *The Dark Knight Rises*. While the post, and the suggestion to mask up, was generally taken in the joking spirit in which it was intended, many of the responses were pretty angry. I can understand that. Nobody wants to know that simply breathing is now a poisonous feminizing activity, even if it's true.

It is true. But that doesn't mean there aren't things we can do—meaningful things—to reduce our exposure to harmful substances, including estrogenic chemicals in the air, even if we can't totally eliminate them from our lives. In this chapter, I'll tell you exactly what you can do to protect yourself from harmful exposures as much as possible and also how you can improve your health and hormonal profile with other simple interventions. Most of this advice won't be sex-specific (we can all benefit from diet, exercise, and better sleep), but I'll be addressing men in particular, and talking about testosterone, because men and testosterone are the subject of the book.

Later I'll discuss some of what's going on at the frontiers of health optimization, among a group of people commonly referred to as "biohackers." Biohacking, and in particular gene therapy, holds immense promise, and more than a little risk, for those looking to improve their health and escape the ravages of the modern world. Biohackers are already using targeted genetic interventions to tweak key processes within the body and trigger the release of substances like klotho, an anti-aging protein, or follistatin, a protein that has been widely shown to increase muscle growth. As expensive as such treatments may be at present, in the future the cost will decrease significantly. Gene therapy may become as common as popping supplements or even replace them and be far more effective.

To find out more about what's happening in the field of biohacking, I spoke to Mac Davis, the founder of Minicircle, a company with a research lab in Texas and gene therapy clinics in the Caribbean and the Middle East. We talked about his company's pioneering follistatin therapy and the future of biohacking for mankind, including gene therapy that specifically targets the body's production of testosterone.

I'll also mention collective solutions to the problems I've identified, including attempts to regulate chemicals in a different way and promote healthier lifestyles. This is where we start to run into further problems, especially if we want to start a movement for masculine revival. I'll talk about my experience as part of the Tucker Carlson documentary *The End of Men*, in 2022. Perhaps more than anything else, the bizarre, hysterical reaction to the documentary in the mainstream media reveals just how hostile the prevailing culture is to men who want to be men.

But the problem of collective solutions, ultimately, runs deeper than liberal talking heads bandying about accusations of closet homosexuality. I'll return to Fukuyama at the end of the book, to consider whether liberal democracy can ever truly accommodate a fully elaborated, satisfying form of masculinity within its boundaries. Fukuyama, at least, saw that the only "solution" to the problem of liberalism's hostility to and elimination of *thymos* was what he called "immense wars of the spirit." This phrase wasn't a euphemism: he really did mean *immense wars*, as men use the most potent and destructive means of expressing their will to bring some form of meaning to life again beyond the endless repetition of consumerism and participation in mass democratic politics.

So What Can We Do? The Individual Response

WHEN IT comes to harmful substances, the best strategies all center around avoidance. Avoid contact with these substances in the first place or reduce your exposure to them as much as you can. Persistent exposure is generally the most important form—we're exposed to the same chemicals again and again and our bodies just never get a break from them—but some chemicals also accumulate within the body, particularly in the fat stores, and getting rid of those is a more difficult prospect.

With regard to plastics and plastic chemicals, lowering your exposure means a number of quite simple practical things. Reduce your use of plastics, in any form, as much as possible. Plastic bottles, plastic bags, plastic tupperware, plastic clothing and furnishings. Processed food, pretty much by definition, comes wrapped in plastic and will be contaminated by plastic and plastic chemicals in the factory as well. For God's sake don't let children gnaw on plastic bottles, toys, pacifiers, or any other kind of plastic object for that matter. Children, especially toddlers, have been shown to have up to ten times more microplastics in their feces than adults because a procession of plastic objects enter their mouths on a daily basis, but also because they spend their lives close to the ground, crawling around in carpets and on floors where microplastics accumulate in dust.[181] That's why you should vacuum your home regularly—the home is where the greatest amount of microplastic exposure occurs for most people—and consider using a HEPA filter to clean the air. Don't chop your food on a plastic cutting board, either. One study claims a plastic cutting board could contribute as much as 50g of microplastics, or five credit cards, to a person's diet every year.[182] Get a wooden board instead. Wooden boards also have natural antimicrobial properties and they look better, too. Commercial kitchens are required to use plastic boards, but you're not.

And if you own a microwave, don't ever heat food in it in a plastic container. Hundreds of chemicals can migrate into food from plastic containers when they're placed in a microwave, as well as huge numbers of microplastics.[183]

Another very powerful thing you can do to reduce your exposure to harmful chemicals is simply to start eating organic. A recent study showed that bodily levels of the chemical glyphosate can be reduced by as much as 43 percent in as little as a week by switching to organic fruit and vegetables.[184] Processed and fast foods are laced with harmful chemicals, because of the poor quality non-organic ingredients they contain. In 2023, the nonprofit Moms Across America commissioned a study of pesticides and other harmful substances in

America's twenty top-selling fast-food brands.[185] Around 85 million Americans eat fast food every day, and many of the chains featured in the study also supply school lunches. 100 percent of samples taken in the study contained glyphosate, with the highest levels—213.58 parts per billion and 225.54 parts per billion—in food from Panera Bread, which markets itself as a "healthy option." Levels of just 0.01 parts per billion can cause liver and organ damage in lab animals. Twenty-seven different pesticides were found in the study samples, with some food containing as many as nine different pesticides. The samples also contained veterinary antibiotics, medicines and hormones, and high levels of heavy metals.

One of the most powerful things you can do to take control of your health is learn how to cook. That's why I chose to make my first book as the Raw Egg Nationalist a cookbook. If you learn how to prepare simple delicious meals at home, including preparing food ahead when you know you're going to be short of time, you can reduce or even totally eliminate your need to rely on corporations or take-out restaurants to prepare your food for you. Eating out regularly is associated with poorer health, and there are lots of studies that show an association between the growth of eating "food away from home" and obesity, not least of all because fast food and restaurant food contains, on average, significantly more calories than a comparable meal prepared at home.[186]

Cookware should also be a focus. Nonstick coatings are often made with toxic PFAS chemicals, such as Teflon, which leach into food. Once the surface of nonstick pans becomes degraded and starts to scratch, it releases millions of microplastic particles into the food.[187] Choose copper, ceramic, or stainless steel cookware instead. If you learn how to cook properly with butter and other fats by controlling the temperature, you won't need a nonstick pan.

Filter your water. This is an obvious one. Contamination of the water supply varies from area to area. Some areas will have some chemicals, others will have different ones, but you can usually expect a soup of herbicides, pesticides, pharmaceuticals, and other nasty things, even if the water has already been treated. All 120 samples of tap water in a nationwide U.S. survey from 2021 had detectable levels of PFAS in them, for example, and 35 percent of the samples had levels above the *Consumer Reports* maximum threshold for safety, which like most thresholds is probably far too high anyway.[188] Well water is just as likely to be contaminated as municipal tap water. You can get a countertop gravity filter that you fill manually or install an under-the-counter activated charcoal and reverse-osmosis system. Whatever you do, do *something*, because the water you drink will be a major source of exposure to harmful chemicals, including endocrine disruptors.

Personal-care products and cleaning products, including things like soaps and air fresheners, are a major source of exposure for men—and especially women. A survey showed that college-age girls in the U.S. use an average of eight products a day—deodorants, conditioners, perfumes, liquid soaps, hand and body lotions, sunscreen, nail polish, eyeshadow, lip balm—that contain endocrine-disrupting chemicals.[189] Some of the girls surveyed used as many as seventeen such products. The effect of simply giving up these products or finding natural alternatives is immediate and significant. If girls go cold turkey on personal-care products, they can reduce levels of harmful chemicals like phthalates, parabens, and phenols in their urine by as much as 45 percent in just three days.[190]

You should also pay attention to the chemicals you use in the garden as well if you have one. Glyphosate isn't just used by soy and corn farmers in the Midwest. It's sold to the general public as Roundup, and applied to gardens and lawns and green spaces across the country by ordinary people. Ditch chemical pesticides, herbicides, and fertilizers and learn permaculture methods to keep on top of weeds and enhance the growth and health of your plants. This will be better for you and your family, and for the wildlife in your garden as well.

The best strategy is to avoid or mitigate exposure. But what about chemicals and harmful substances already in the body? Can we remove them, too?

This is a more difficult question. People want to know about microplastics in particular because of the horrifying studies that show they're in our eyes and brains and balls and pretty much every internal organ. Can I get the microplastics out of my balls? The simple answer is, we don't know yet. It's likely there are natural mechanisms that remove microplastics from our bodies, but what they are, and whether we can enhance or supplement them, isn't clear at this point. Microplastic research is too young right now, but I'm sure in a few years we'll have a much better idea.

Other harmful substances like BPA and phthalates can be removed. We know that sweating, whether through exercise or the use of a sauna, can effectively mobilize harmful substances stored in the body's tissues, including the skin and fat. When people are tested for phthalates, for example, with blood, sweat, and urine samples, levels of the chemicals are higher in the sweat than in the blood or urine.[191] This suggests that stored phthalates are excreted more readily in sweat. Sauna-based detoxing has already been shown to be effective in cases of chronic illness caused by methamphetamine exposure.[192]

Because many harmful substances are lipophilic—meaning they end up in fat tissue—calorie restriction, and therefore fat loss, is another important means of cleansing the body, when combined with strenuous exercise or time in the sauna. Evidence suggests that when the body's fat tissues are metabolized, harmful substances stored within them are transferred to the skin, making it easier for them to pass out of the body via sweat.[193]

It's also possible to remove certain substances by having blood drawn regularly. Firefighters are exposed to a wide variety of harmful substances in the line of duty, including PFAS chemicals in foams and retardants, and as a result they accumulate sickeningly high levels in their bodies. In Australia, 285 firefighters, all but six of whom were male, were enrolled in a year-long trial in which they gave plasma every six weeks, blood every twelve weeks, or did neither.[194] Those who gave blood or plasma saw significant reductions in their blood levels of PFAS. Plasma donation proved to be wildly effective, reducing levels of certain PFAS compounds by as much as three times the amount of blood donation. This is also one of the reasons why women generally seem to have lower levels of PFAS in their blood. For decades they give blood once a month—through menstruation. Women may, on average, have 25 percent lower levels of PFAS in their blood than men simply because they're constantly losing blood.[195]

Simple Changes Matter

HERE ARE some broader points about optimizing your health. Diet, exercise, and sleep should, in my opinion, be your three main focuses. Men who believe they have low testosterone increasingly reach straight for testosterone-replacement therapy—artificial testosterone administered by a physician—in the belief that this is the only way to solve their problem, but of course it isn't. Some of this may also be laziness and our collective belief that the solution to every health problem is or should be a pill or medical treatment. By all means, speak to a physician if you believe you have low testosterone. There are congenital forms of low testosterone, and you may have one and require artificial testosterone to replace what your body can't produce. It's unlikely, though. What's more likely, in fact what's almost certain, is that your lifestyle is sub-optimal and a few determined changes will be enough, over a period of time, to put you back on the right track.

Weight loss works. Obese men who lose weight see a significant increase in their male reproductive parameters across the board: testosterone and other hormones, sperm count, and sperm quality.[196] What's important to remember is that you should be looking to lose weight only if you're overweight. Weight loss is actually associated with testosterone *decreases* if you're already a decent weight: anybody who has undertaken a severe "cut" to get the most chiselled body possible will know this.[197] Professional bodybuilders waddle onto the stage on contest-day with the hormonal profile of a famine-stricken 90-year-old woman.

Exercise is essential. That doesn't necessarily mean a determined regimen of weight training, either, although I recommend it as a means of building the most muscle and increasing your testosterone the most. For overweight men, simply becoming more active by walking briskly or jogging, in combination with a calorie-restriction diet, is enough to raise testosterone levels. When overweight middle-aged Japanese men combined a calorie-restriction diet with brisk walking or running three times a week for twelve weeks, they lost an average of almost 12 kg and increased their testosterone, as well as improving other health parameters like their insulin sensitivity and blood lipids.[198] Nobody is so busy they can't go for a brisk walk three times a week.

Muscle: A Key to Masculine Health

IN THE long term, one of the best strategies for maintaining good health, including healthy levels of body fat, is to build muscle. This is because muscle is more metabolically expensive tissue than any other kind, so it protects you from the negative effects of overeating. If you stop exercising, the more muscle tissue you have, the more you'll have to eat to get into a calorie surplus and put on fat tissue. It's often the case that people who lose a lot of weight through running or other intense cardiovascular exercise "rebound" dramatically as soon as they stop. Whether intense long-term cardiovascular exercise causes muscle loss is a moot point, but there's no question that it doesn't build muscle in anything like the same way as weight training. When determined runners or cyclists return to their old bad habits after losing weight, they don't have the same metabolic insurance, if you will, as somebody who has built a muscular body that requires more calories to maintain at rest.

Don't get me wrong. If you overeat, you put on weight, regardless of whether you have a body like Lance Armstrong or a body like Arnold Schwarzenegger circa 1975. It's simple thermodynamics. What I'm saying is that one of muscle's many useful functions is to provide a hedge against weight gain when you take the foot off the gas. You'll have to get back to lifting weights reasonably sharpish, though, if you want to maintain that muscle.

Ozempic: All That Glitters Is Not Gold

THIS IS probably a good place to talk about the new weight-loss medications like Wegovy/Ozempic and Mounjaro. If you're seriously obese and unable to exercise in a determined manner, it may very well be the case that a drug like Wegovy/Ozempic is the best option. Users of these drugs should beware, however, that one of the principal effects of using them is muscle loss. Almost all of the studies of these drugs—and especially the headline-grabbing trials funded by the companies that manufacture them—fail to distinguish between the *type* of weight lost—i.e., whether the subjects have lost valuable tissue that really ought to be preserved (muscle and even bone) or fat. Anecdotal evidence worrying enough to make the national media suggests a significant proportion of long-term weight loss with Wegovy and competitor drugs is muscle and lean tissue, at a far greater rate than would be expected with good old-fashioned weight loss built on calorie restriction and exercise.[199] Not only does this leave people weaker than they should be after weight loss, but it sets them up for a significant rebound if they return to their old habits.

Think very carefully before using these new drugs. You should also be aware of the risk of side effects up to and including death in some cases. The less serious side effects include permanent stomach paralysis, uncontrollable diarrhea, and the still-unexplored potential for thyroid tumors. Pretty much all GLP-1 receptor agonists—that's the class of drug to which Wegovy/Ozempic belongs—reliably induce thyroid tumors in rodents when they're used in the longer term.[200] It's been an unspoken assumption with these drugs that most users will have to stay on them, perhaps even permanently, in order to maintain a healthy weight, which is good news for the manufacturers' shareholders at least.

Stop Being Vegan!

EATING PROPERLY is, of course, essential to being healthy and building muscle. Ditch processed food, as I've already suggested, and favor high-quality, nutrient-dense animal foods to provide the protein, fats, vitamins, minerals, and micronutrients your body needs. Learn to cook and you won't need other people to prepare your food for you.

If you're a vegan or vegetarian, go back and re-read what I wrote in the last chapter about the inadequacy of plant-based diets. I understand the ethical arguments for vegetarianism and veganism, by which I mean the arguments about animal welfare, but you have to understand that you were not meant to be a herbivore, as Weston Price established definitively, beyond all question, in *Nutrition and Physical Degeneration*. At the very least, introduce eggs and dairy into your diet. Lacto-ovo vegetarians generally don't suffer the health problems that vegetarians, and especially vegans, suffer because they still get cholesterol and saturated fat, superior animal protein, and a wealth of nutrients and micronutrients that plant-based eaters miss out on. Indeed, lacto-ovo vegetarians can build extraordinary physiques. Bill Pearl, the champion bodybuilder, became one later in his career and still looked fantastic.

If you're worried about animal welfare (you should be), just make sure you buy the best quality local products. Perhaps there's a local farm you can go to, like I do, to get your eggs and milk, where you can see the cows and chickens living the happy, outdoor lives their nature demands.

Here isn't the place to lay out the intricacies of dieting for fat loss or muscle gain—actually, it's not that hard—but I will say that your eating needs to match your stated goals. If you want to lose weight, you can't do that in a calorie surplus, and you'll not build muscle, generally, in a calorie deficit, unless your body is drawing on ample fat stores (this is called "body recomposition"). You will probably have to draw up a diet plan. Even if you're just looking to maintain the same weight, you should pay close attention to what you eat. But you can also use simpler, more intuitive methods that don't require calculation or the weighing of food. I track my weight simply by use of a mirror and scale and adjust my intake according to whether I like what I see. This is successful, I think, because I tend to eat the same foods day-in and day-out. Regular variation and lots of eating out would make it much harder.

The Essential Ingredient: Sleep

ONE VERY important aspect of your lifestyle that should be addressed with urgency is sleep. Sleep is absolutely crucial for good health, including proper hormonal function, across the board. Chronic disturbances to sleep, which are particularly visible in shift workers, can have disastrous effects on health. "Circadian misalignment," when the body's natural day-and-night rhythms are thrown out of whack, has significant knock-on effects on the body's ability to manage eating and weight, for example. Just a few days of shift work are enough to alter the body's production of key proteins involved in the regulation of appetite, metabolism, and blood sugar levels.[201] It's well known that nurses who do night shifts are fatter than nurses who work during the day.[202] But even if you aren't working night shifts at hospitals, losing sleep or getting poor-quality sleep will impact your health significantly. People who sleep only five hours a night as opposed to seven or eight hours a night gain weight twice as fast, according to one large-scale study of over 70,000 women.[203] It's reckoned at least 30 percent of adults don't get the recommended seven or more hours of sleep a night, and maybe as little as 15 percent of adults get at least five nights a week of between seven and nine hours.[204]

Men produce most of their testosterone at night, so if you want to optimize your testosterone levels, you'll need to take your sleep seriously. A small amount of acute sleep deprivation doesn't seem to make a huge difference, but chronic deprivation causes serious reductions.[205] Just eight days of five hours' sleep a night can reduce the testosterone levels of men in their twenties by as much as 15 percent, or one-sixth.[206] Another study, by the researcher Plamen Penev suggests that doubling your sleep from four hours a night to eight could double your testosterone, at least if you're an older man (over 64).[207] One of the reasons why older men tend to have less testosterone than younger men seems to be that older men tend to sleep worse. This is very well documented.

Sleep appears to have powerful anti-estrogenic effects. For example, the anti-estrogenic substance tamoxifen, which is given to women with estrogen-sensitive breast cancer, stops working on rats with cancer that are exposed to light at night.[208] Giving melatonin to the rats makes the tamoxifen work. Melatonin, a substance that is mostly secreted during healthy sleep by the pineal gland, has been shown to have a strong inhibitory effect on aromatase, the enzyme that's responsible for converting testosterone in the body to estrogen.[209]

It's not a wonder, then, that researchers believe poor sleep may be an essential, and largely neglected, factor in the epidemic of low testosterone. One study, which showed that adding just an hour of sleep a night could boost testosterone levels by 12 percent, concluded that men with low androgen concentrations should be subject to "an evaluation of their sleep hygiene" as a matter of course.[210]

"Sleep hygiene" refers to the preparations we take before we go to sleep and the environment we sleep in. Addressing your sleep hygiene and doing things like reducing your exposure to light in the evening, especially blue light from electronic devices, is the best way to guarantee good sleep. Creating a calming, natural routine and establishing regularity—a set time to go to bed and wake up—is particularly important. There are also a number of "hacks" you can use to make it easier to go to sleep, such as taking a warm shower or bath before bed—a meta-study of eleven sleep studies showed that doing so halves the length of time it takes to fall asleep once you're in bed[211]— and exercising outside in the sun during the day, which also appears to halve the length of time it takes to fall asleep.[212]

I've outlined what I consider to be the most important ways you can fight back against the estrogenic burden of modern life and improve your health as a man: avoiding toxic exposures in the first place, detoxing your body, weight loss, exercise; improving your diet, and improving your sleep. Get on these things carefully over a period of time and I can promise your life will get measurably better. In the longer term, your life will be unrecognizable.

The Frontiers of Health Optimization: Biohacking for Masculine Revival

BUT THE future—indeed, the present, if you have the money—holds the potential for even more powerful interventions on an individual level. Biohacking, as it's often called, involves a wide variety of different techniques, including gene therapy, to open new horizons of hormonal health, longevity and physical performance.

Mac Davis has created a company called Minicircle and a chain of special clinics across the Caribbean devoted to improving health with cutting-edge technology. Minicircle offers a pioneering follistatin gene therapy treatment that promises enhanced muscle growth, reduced fat mass, and increased longevity for those who can afford it. In the future they're looking to have a wider variety of treatments, including testosterone gene therapy that could, conceivably, increase a person's testosterone levels to the upper end of the natural limit, or even beyond it.

My plan had been to fly to the Caribbean to one of Mac's clinics, and maybe even to have his new follistatin gene therapy treatment while I was there. Mac had offered me the treatment the first time we spoke. I pictured myself arriving by small jet, like something from a Michael Mann film, in a tasteful linen suit and, maybe, with a not-so-tasteful mustache grown just for the occasion.

But as it turns out, I'm talking to Mac on Skype and doing my best to find a camera angle and lighting that doesn't make me look like a serial killer. So it goes.

Mac is a cool guy. Very laid back, knows his stuff, as you'd hope, but doesn't bash you over the head with science. Totally open to challenge and to different ways of thinking about issues, but also firm in his convictions and not afraid to defend them vigorously.

I think to myself how different medicine would be if it were full of people like Mac Davis.

Biohacking, as it's called, is now reckoned to be a multi-billion-dollar business. I've read estimates that the scene is worth as much as $60 billion worldwide, mostly in the U.S., but there are also high-end clinics across the world wherever there is money, including Monaco, Jeddah, and Dubai.

It's hard to pin down exactly what biohacking is and draw a clean line between it and other forms of health optimization. After all, high technology and science have been applied to health and physical performance for some time now. Think of the Soviet Olympic doping program as depicted in *Rocky IV*'s Ivan Drago, a chemically enhanced, technologically honed *Übermensch*.

But the general consensus is that whatever biohacking is and whoever biohackers are, the people themselves are all united by a "propensity for self-experimentation that, to some, might seem a little off," to use the words of *Wired* magazine.[213] These are people who are pushing the limits of what's possible, and going far beyond what any doctor, mainstream health professional, or the FDA would advocate.

According to Alex Azzi, a Dubai businessman who runs the website biohack.ae, which sells a wide range of health products from MCT oil—that's medium-chain triglyceride oil, if you didn't know—to mushrooms:

> "Part of the biohacker philosophy is finding shortcuts to improve performance. Healthy living is something our parents would do; biohacking is a different spin. It's finding ingenious ways to solve old problems. It's a systems approach to life, which includes getting the most out of the least."

Azzi stresses that biohacking isn't just about the high tech:

> "There is a big movement to ancestral wisdom. We have become domesticated creatures. We are the poodles of our species. We have to get in touch with the wilder, more primal parts of ourselves. When we put a system under stress, the system gets stronger."

He adds that "in the biohacker community, there is zero support for bad ideas," which I find pretty hard to believe, frankly.

The movement is often divided into subcultures. There are transhumanists, who want to become cyborgs, a mixture of flesh and machine; grinders, do-it-yourself experimenters who do things like implanting RFID chips under their skin so they can control electronic devices or injecting chemicals into their eyes to give themselves night vision; primitivists, who advocate a return to lifestyles of the distant pre-industrial past; and so-called pragmatists, who want to use new technologies and treatments to help the sick, disabled, and poor.

As I write those definitions, it strikes me that I could probably be called a primitivist, with my emphasis on returning to ancestral diets and lifestyles—following the earth's diurnal rhythms, exposing yourself to the elements and the changing seasons, shielding yourself from excessive blue light and the toxic products of modern industrial science—but then again I don't believe in a total return to tradition. The modern world has its benefits, not least of all Microsoft Word. And books.

Suffice to say, some people would probably call me a biohacker too and class me with dudes like Brian Johnson, a.k.a. the Liver King, who has built a system of "Nine Ancestral Tenets" based on practices like maximizing sleep, eating whole foods, and spending time outdoors when exercising. The one tenet the Liver King forgot to mention, as we discovered, was taking huge quantities of anabolic substances, including $10,000 worth of human growth hormone a month. Like I said, the modern world has its benefits.

Trying Not to Die

PERHAPS THE most famous biohacker today is another Bryan Johnson—that's Bryan with a "y"—a man who boasts of being "the world's most measured human." Johnson says he spends two million dollars a year on his extensive health regimen, which includes a specially formulated plant-based diet, a raft of supplements and procedures, such as blood transfusions from his teenage son, and exercises designed to increase specific biomarkers associated with longevity, like the VO2 max (maximum oxygen uptake during exercise).

Even if you don't know him by name, you probably know who Bryan Johnson is. He's that *weird* guy, the one who's spent all that money to make himself look like an android out of the Alien franchise. Weird has kind of become his brand, and he doesn't care. In fact, he embraces it.

> Bryan Johnson knows that you think he's weird. So much of his life occurs outside the realms of what most people consider normal that it would be odd if you didn't. He rises at 4.30am, eats all his meals before 11am, and goes to bed— alone—at 8.30pm, without exception. In the intervening hours, he ingests more than 100 pills, bathes his body in LED light, and sits on a high-intensity electromagnetic device that he believes will strengthen his pelvic floor. This is all done in the service of slowing his rate of ageing until, he hopes, one year of chronological time can pass while his biological age stays the same. His ultimate goal? "Don't die."[214]

"Don't die" has become his motto.

Johnson can do all of this because he has a lot of money. In 2013 he sold his company, Braintree Venmo, to Paypal for $800 million. But the money didn't improve his life. In fact, by his account it made it far worse, and he spent the better part of the next ten years eating too much, drinking too much, and generally feeling like shit. And then, two years ago, he snapped out of it and decided to apply an optimization algorithm to his own life. The result is what you see on social media, in the news, and in newspaper weekend magazines.

The world's most measured human is also creating a system he calls "Blueprint," which he'll be releasing at some point as an app, so that other people can do exactly as he does and, presumably, achieve the same results. You can already use a beta version of Blueprint online, on Johnson's website (protocol.bryanjohnson.com). Like many of the leading figures within the biohacking movement, Johnson is vocal about his commitment to democratizing biohacking and ensuring that other people can reap the benefits of the protocol he has come up with at far lower cost. He says that he wants to take the pain out of improving your life and the discipline required. "We're insane right now in that we're addicted to addiction: food, porn, social media, alcohol, whatever," he says. "Blueprint is about acknowledging that it's not reasonable to ask the individual to get their shit together when they've got a thousand things within two miles of them that have heroin-like dopamine highs."

Bryan Johnson is probably the most high-profile person to have had Minicircle's follistatin treatment, apart from the arm-wrestler Devon Larratt. Johnson detailed his experience with the therapy and its effects in a social-media video he posted in June 2024.[215] The video follows him as he travels to Minicircle's clinic in Roatan, an island off the coast of Honduras, to experience what he describes as "an extreme medical procedure that could change the future of humanity."

The clinic is situated in Próspera, a special economic zone modelled on Singapore, Dubai, and Hong Kong. Billed as the "world's first startup city," it has its own fiscal, legal, and regulatory systems designed to attract investment and innovation that would not be possible under standard government frameworks. The zone has its own ruling council and civil law. Residents must sign a special social contract and pay an annual fee. Bitcoin is legal tender. Investors in the project include tech luminaries Balaji Srinivasan, Peter Thiel, and Marc Andreessen.

Startup cities aside, according to Bryan Johnson, gene therapy might be the answer to the longevity ceiling of 120 years placed on human life. The idea behind all gene therapy is basically the same: genetic material is introduced into the body and incorporated into the organism's own genetic makeup. This can be done in order to fix a faulty gene, replace one that's missing or even introduce a totally new gene the organism didn't have before. It can also be done to turn genes on or off. Which genes are introduced or targeted depends on the effects that are sought. Gene therapy is already licensed by the FDA and used to treat a number of different conditions, such as cancer, cystic fibrosis, and hemophilia, but for most people the closest they're likely to get to it is as part of a clinical trial—if they're lucky.

Johnson says he has avoided gene therapy up until now because it seemed "too risky." "If a therapy caused, say, cancer in my body, there would be nothing I could do to reverse the process," he says in the video. Minicircle's therapy is different, however, because it has a "built-in kill-switch," which allows it to be turned off at will. The common antibiotic tetracycline can be taken to destroy the DNA molecules used for the procedure. If those molecules are destroyed, the follistatin gene therapy stops.

Johnson's 71-year-old father also received the therapy. Johnson has frequently expressed concern about his father's lifestyle and the fact that his actual life expectancy, measured through epigenetic factors and other bodily processes, is three years less than his current age.

When it comes to the results, Bryan Johnson is impressed. He says that his speed of aging has "dropped to 0.64 (a personal best)," meaning "I now celebrate my birthday every 19 months;" his "muscle mass is up by 7 percent (already in the 99th percentile);" and his follistatin levels increased by 160 percent in the two weeks after the injection. In short, his body is aging slower and he has significantly more muscle."

The Follistatin Journey

WHEN I talk to Mac Davis, it's a while before we get on to Bryan Johnson, but we do eventually. We start by talking about the general motivation behind biohacking and why it may be inevitable in the current environment, given the unprecedented degree to which we have created a toxic environment for ourselves over the last century.

"We can do things to reduce pollutants, but the microplastics are already in our balls. We need something else to fight back. I think the answer is gene therapy and the democratization of gene therapy that's coming to society very soon." Gene therapy, Mac says, will "allow people to choose their own endocrine metabolism [hormone function] to a very fine degree." This doesn't mean Mac believes there is nothing people can do to improve their lives and health without gene therapy, or that the problem of environmental pollution can't be addressed. Mac simply believes gene therapy is an enormously powerful new kind of intervention that could soon be in the hands of thousands or millions of people, allowing them to control their hormone levels and fine tune them in a way that was simply impossible before.

Mac believes there needs to be a political movement to clean up the environment and to regulate harmful chemicals, but we both agree that this is going to take a long time to bear fruit, probably decades.

Mac is keen to point out, though, that gene therapy of this kind is not totally revolutionary, even if it uses technology that, until only a few decades ago, didn't even exist. "Intentional hormone modification" is not new, he says.

> "Historically, the first major hormones that were discovered that really altered society were testosterone and estrogen. People started experimenting with altering those right away. So you got anabolic steroids, testosterone-replacement therapy, and oral contraceptives." Gene therapy is just "the next stage in attempting to intentionally modify the human endocrine system."

Biohackers are like primitive shamans or medicine men, Mac continues. They were the "scientific empiricists" of their time, as biohackers are today, wandering the forests and searching for different plants and substances to heal wounds, increase libido or even enhance the connection to the spiritual realm or gods. I'm pretty sure that image is how a lot of biohackers picture themselves.

We talk about Minicircle's clientele. Is it just people like Bryan Johnson—that is, wealthy Americans? Johnson says the follistatin treatment cost him $20,000, which is obviously beyond the price range of most people. Mac admits that, yes, it's mostly "tech entrepreneurs," 75 percent male, between the ages of 35 and 75, mostly from the U.S.; although, at the time of our interview, Minicircle was about to open a clinic in Dubai, which is likely to expand its client base. Mac is keen to emphasize that he wants to treat as many people as possible from all different backgrounds. "I want to make the best genes available to more people," he says.

In total, Minicircle has treated 350 people. "No significant side effects," Mac tells me proudly.

We talk in detail about the follistatin treatment and how it works. Mac walks me through the whole process as if I were a new client. First there'd be a telemedicine call with a physician to discuss my health records and ensure I was a good fit. This first stage would be essential to ensure my health and expectations were in order. If that call went well, I'd fly to Roatan and get picked up at the airport by one of the clinic staff. Once I'm at the clinic, the treatment itself wouldn't take long: thirty seconds for the administration of the genetic material by a single subcutaneous injection with a needle. That's it. Congratulations: I'd be a genetically enhanced person.

Mac explains the technicalities:

> "Prior to injection, the physician will mix the plasmid DNA with a cationic polymer that complexes with the DNA and helps it to be absorbed by the cell and transported to the nucleus. Once the DNA goes to the nucleus, the cell starts to code for the hormone follistatin, which is then secreted into the blood and travels around the body, where it signals to the body's tissues in various different ways, including to increase the synthesis of muscle fibers."

It's not actually that complicated to understand: the therapy is simply providing instructions (a plasmid) for the body's cells to produce a specific protein (follistatin), which in turn provides instructions to the body's tissues to do various things, like build muscle.

Mac reminds me again that the treatment is reversible. If something goes wrong, the plasmids can be destroyed within the body using the common antibiotic tetracycline. That's how simple it is.

Okay. So I've had the treatment. What then? How will I feel?

"The first feeling is typically one of increased vitality. Just a general sense of increased energy and well-being. It takes about four days after the therapy for the body to reach the maximum amount of follistatin secretion. That's when the effects first hit for our clients." Beyond that, Mac says, clients notice greater strength, a closer "mind-muscle connection"—the sense of being in direct mental control of the muscles that bodybuilders covet so much—and more endurance. He also says that clients recover faster from exercise and heal better. Some of Minicircle's clients have the treatment specifically for rehabilitation of various kinds of injuries. Mac says the treatment is proving particularly effective for sufferers of rheumatoid arthritis, some of whom have "experienced complete cessation of symptoms for about four months after the treatment, and then a significant reduction in pain over the next year."

"Mostly, right now," Mac says, "the treatment is for people seeking longevity. Everything else they could do, they've done. They've already had their diet together for ten years. They already exercise daily or pretty much. They're fit. They have good body composition. They already try a wide variety of supplements and they've been through blood testing and various kinds of functional medicine. This is just the next step for them, the last thing they can do that they just haven't tried."

So why isn't Mac offering this treatment in the U.S.? Why Prospera, off the coast of Honduras? Minicircle has a research lab in Austin, Texas, but no treatment facilities there. Would Minicircle even be able to offer this treatment in the U.S.?

The answer is no, and it has to do with the way the FDA regulates medical treatments. Mac tells me the FDA wants treatments for people who are sick, and for particular specified illnesses, but as he's just explained, most of his clients aren't sick. If anything, they're in the peak of health and they want to get even better. The FDA won't even accept sarcopenia—age-related muscle loss, which is a key indicator of mortality—as a valid condition. They want treatments for conditions like limb-girdle muscular dystrophy, which none of Mac's clients or potential clients have or probably ever will have.

And then there's the micromanagement. Mac and his team are used to having new ideas, testing them, and putting them to use therapeutically in a short amount of time. The FDA would want oversight of each new iteration in a way that would make rapid advancement impossible. In Prospera, Minicircle can make small changes quickly but still respect and ensure the informed consent of its patients. Clients are given full disclosure and allowed to choose on the basis of the information they're given.

Although follistatin gene therapy has been carried out on animals for over a quarter of century, none of that data would be considered valid by the FDA. The safety and success of those treatments would count for nothing. It would be back to square one, with the FDA watching every single step. Minicircle would have to assemble a totally fresh portfolio of studies, starting with its own animal trials. This is something every company is required to do with a new therapy.

"If we were doing this in the U.S. right now, we'd probably be having calls with the FDA every six months and doing tests on animals and going back and forth trying to get approval to test our therapy on humans." It would be "years" before somebody like Bryan Johnson could walk into their clinic, get an injection, and walk out, regardless of what Minicircle or Bryan Johnson wanted.

Mac has big dreams for the future. He explains that gene therapy has the potential to be used cheaply as part of public-health interventions for thousands or millions of people. He tells me about klotho, which he calls the "current darling of the longevity community." Klotho has many effects, but among its most important is regulation of calcium and phosphate deposits within the body's tissues. Arteries calcify, kidney stones form and, in the brain, "sand" appears—all of these things cause aging, decline, and disease. Mac believes administration of klotho on a wide scale could have dramatic effects on cognitive function at a societal level, perhaps even as dramatically as the iodinization of salt, which prevented an epidemic of cognitive dysfunction in places like Switzerland, where iodine deficiencies were common. In some places, there was a twelve-point IQ increase—one whole standard deviation. Mac hails this as "one of the greatest public health benefits of all time, with no side effects or externalities." Although Minicircle doesn't currently offer klotho gene therapy, other clinics do.

Gene Therapy and You

GENE THERAPY is a hugely powerful technology, I can see that, and it's going to get more powerful. Powerful technology is often jealously guarded. Couldn't gene therapy just as easily be used by a narrow elite to increase the gulf between themselves and the rest of the population? Could pre-existing social divisions, which are already in part biological divisions, become the basis for a genuine biological separation within the human race—an eloi and morlocks situation, like in H.G. Wells' *The Time Machine*? Imagine the ultra-rich endowing themselves and their offspring with 200+ IQ and a body capable of Olympic performance, while the great mass of people sink deeper into metabolic, hormonal, and cognitive dysfunction, obesity, and chronic illness.

"Democratization of gene therapy is inevitable," Mac responds confidently, with barely a pause. Costs are already coming down significantly, and that trend will continue. The treatment Bryan Johnson paid $20,000 for will cost a fraction of that within a few years. The only things that will prevent the uptake of gene therapy are individual choice—people deciding they don't want the therapy for whatever reason—and governments preventing people from having access to it. That's it, Mac says. I'm not fully convinced, but his optimism is infectious. Time will tell.

I almost forgot: What about testosterone? If Minicircle is targeting men who want to improve their health and performance, why follistatin and not testosterone? Surely testosterone is the marquee product.

Mac says Minicircle started with follistatin because there's such a long history of testing and treatment with follistatin therapy. That's generally the model for how Minicircle chooses therapies: the process begins with a deep dive into the published scientific literature to find animal studies that suggest a treatment could work in humans. This gives Minicircle a "running start." The problem with testosterone therapy, Mac says, is that treatments for testosterone deficiencies generally haven't focused on gene therapy. Instead, they've focused on the administration of exogeneous hormones (i.e., hormones from outside the body), so Minicircle has had to start from scratch. The clinic is working on a testosterone therapy, but the mechanism of action—how it actually achieves an increase in testosterone production within the body—requires tweaking. The interaction between the various hormones that work to control testosterone balance within the body is more complicated than first expected. Mac is confident, though, that Minicircle will have a product ready soon, and that it will be extremely popular.

Maybe next time, if we meet in Roatan, I'll take him up on his offer and try the gene therapy. Mac and I agreed on plenty, not least of all the fact that the assaults of the modern world on our bodies, including endocrine disruptors, must be fought off by individuals themselves and by broader political movements. Individuals should do all they can to protect themselves, and that might include biohacking, but there also needs to be a group and institutional response as well.

The question is what the wider response might be and whether it's likely to happen. How can we address these problems collectively?

Can we?

Beyond the Individual Response: Opportunities and Problems

I'VE ALREADY detailed the insanity of the current regulatory system for chemicals and food additives in the U.S. I've suggested that "harmful until proven otherwise" should be our new approach if we really want to do something about the burden of toxicity in the environment and our food and water supply. We simply can't assume that chemicals and additives are safe after little to no testing and then act years or even decades later once overwhelming evidence of their harm has accrued—evidence that can, nevertheless, be disputed by powerful interests that want the pollution and harm to continue because it's profitable. Taking that short-sighted approach is why we're in this dreadful mess in the first place. It needs to change.

So again, what can be done? Well, we can start by reforming institutions like the FDA, which has control over the system of food additives, and the EPA and USDA, and ensuring they operate independently of the industries they're supposed to regulate, under new guidelines that pri-oritize the health of the people, rather than the profits of corporations and the scientists, bureaucrats, and politicians in their pockets.

What I'm advocating isn't simply a movement to restore health. I'm also backing a movement of *masculine* health—a masculine revival. Defeating corrupt corporate and regula-tory interests won't be easy, for sure, but neither will creat-ing a large-scale movement to get men of all ages, but espe-cially young men, to take control of their lives, get active and raise their testosterone. If you want proof of that, just look at the reaction to the Tucker Carlson documentary *The End of Men*, which I starred in back in 2022, alongside a cast of fellow "right-wing bodybuilders" from Twitter and Robert F. Kennedy Jr. himself.

In many ways, this book is a follow-on to that documen-tary. *The End of Men* focused on the precipitous decline in testosterone and fertility among men in recent decades. It opened with a John F. Kennedy speech about "chubby little fat children" and how a nation is only as strong as the people it is made up of, interspersed with footage of the famous La Sierra High School fitness program, which Kennedy wanted to roll out across the nation and probably would have if he hadn't been killed. The documentary interviewed repro-ductive-health experts, including Professor Shanna Swan, to establish the extent of the decline in masculine health and vitality as measured through sperm counts and testosterone levels, and looked at some of the main causes, especially endocrine-disrupting chemicals, sedentary lifestyles and bad diet. The second half of the documentary took an amazing, surreal swerve as the focus turned to the efforts of right-wing bodybuilders, including myself and my friends William Wheelwright (another anon), Dan Lyman, and others, to kick against the pricks and actually do something about the problems outlined in the first half. The entire second half of the documentary focused on us, and all the things we do to fortify our bodies and minds and resist masculine decline.

The End of Men (the Documentary)

THE DOCUMENTARY involved filming action scenes at Alex Jones's Texas ranch—shooting bottles of vegetable oil with a .50 cal rifle, wrestling and lifting weights, and—perhaps infamously—sunning our balls. We knew the finished product was going to draw a lot of attention. That's what the producers and Tucker Carlson wanted. One of the producers told me that Tucker couldn't stop laughing during the first private screening. "I can't believe I'm being paid to make stuff like this!" he said. It was quite clear to me that my long monologue about "soy globalism"—the current social and political dispensation, the opposite of raw egg nationalism—would ruffle a few feathers, too. Any sugges-tion that health is political, and that ill health might be a form of social control was bound to attract cries of "con-spiracy theory!" and "misinformation!"—especially since we were still in the middle of a pandemic.

But none of us were quite prepared for the reaction when the trailer for the documentary was finally released in the spring of 2022. After a somber, foreboding introduction, we hear the triumphant strains of *Thus Spake Zarathustra*—and suddenly, there, atop a rock, is an anonymous right-wing bodybuilder, arms and legs spread in the Vitruvian Man pose, a JOOV red-light machine pointed directly at his balls. An unforgettable image. Then we are introduced to other right-wing bodybuilders, and a provocative section of my monologue about "iron sharpening iron" and "hard times creating strong men" closes out the trailer.

Reaction to the trailer was borderline hysterical, and among left-liberals it focused entirely on the supposed homoeroticism of the second half. This was no accident.

"I thought I was straight until I watched this. Thank you, Tucker Carlson, thank you"—one typical response on social media. Cenk Uygur, presenter of the Young Turks and a man who has advocated for bestiality, wondered whether there was "some chance Tucker is trolling his own audience because there's gay porn less gay than this."

"I am sitting here next to my gay husband living my gay life reading a gay novel as research for my new gay book," commented New York writer and gay man Mark Harris, "and yet I am not and will never be as gay as whatever is haunting Tucker Carlson's gay fantasies."

Star Trek veteran George Takei simply tweeted, "This is so gay." And George would know.

Hit pieces began appearing by the end of the day and continued steadily for weeks. "Tucker Carlson exposes his insecurities in 'The End of Men' Trailer" (Forbes). "Tucker Carlson's documentary trailer is a bizarre, homoerotic fever dream nobody asked for" (Pink News). "Can Tucker Carlson's bizarrely beefy 'End of Men' teaser be real?" (Los Angeles Magazine). Even Snopes.com thought it necessary to publish a fact-checking piece to confirm that, yes, the End of Men trailer was real and not a parody.

Then came the television talking heads. "A refreshing display of homoeroticism," quipped Stephen Colbert on the *Late Show*. A little strange that Tucker is into the idea of "testicle tanning," Colbert added, since "the last time I checked, he is the whitest dick ever." Seth Meyers and others offered commentary that was just as hilarious and incisive.

The Fag Interpretation of History

IT'S A very familiar, tiresome trope: Calling anything "gay" that looks like traditional masculinity is not a new thing. It's done for reasons that are not difficult to understand. I've called this the "fag interpretation of history," in a nod to the great historian Herbert Butterfield and his "Whig inter-pretation of history." Basically, where the Whig interpreta-tion of history sees everywhere and at all times a movement towards the sunny uplands of Progress, the fag interpreta-tion sees a constant movement out of the closet towards open faggotry. In a piece for the *American Mind*, I described what the fag interpretation does when it's applied rigorously to, well, everything:

> No male historical figure or event involving men or a manly grouping is safe from queering, whether we're talking about Julius Caesar or Alexander the Great, the Spartan last stand at Thermopylae, cowboys, pirates, gang members, or even the simplest masculine pleasures and pastimes. Someone, somewhere, whether they are a tenured academic or an arm-chair psychologist, will always be ready to tell you that the

Spartans fought to the last man because they were all gay lovers; that great historical figure X was driven to make his vast conquests by a repressed desire for a male schoolfriend; or that Brazilian jiu-jitsu is just barely disguised dry humping. Checkmate, bigots![216]

Wherever you turn you'll find someone, be they a tenured academic or an armchair psychologist at a dinner party, to tell you you've got it all wrong. Didn't you know Achilles and Patroclus were *actually* gay lovers? Well, they were. How do I know this? Well, they're men and they're awfully close, and you know what that means . . . As far as self-confirming theories go, it's a strong one. All that's required is for two or more men to do things together.

There are plenty of variations on this theme too. The "small penis" theory of history is one of them, in which the principal motivation for seeking any kind of power—for any expression of *thymos* and especially *megalothymia*—is having a small penis. You've probably heard this one in ordinary conversation, but the media and gossip-rags love it too, and it makes its way into written biographies all the time. Napoleon, Hitler, Donald Trump, Vladimir Putin— all of these men were or are driven by having a small penis. But it's not just seeking power. It's any form of assertive, masculine behavior. Do you like guns? You have a small penis. Do you like big cars? Small penis. And so on, and so on.

A proxy for the small penis theory is the sexual dysfunction theory, where if the man in question isn't accused of having a small penis directly, he is accused of being a massive pervert. We see this with speculation about Hitler's sexual relationships, including with his niece, and of course Donald Trump was accused of paying Russian prostitutes to urinate on him in a hotel room that had previously been occupied by the Obamas.

I'm not sure where this tendency originated. It would be easy—perhaps too easy—to blame Freud. The Viennese Witch Doctor certainly helped make sexuality the great fascination of 20th-century thinking. The fusion of Freud and Marx was key to the development of 20th-century leftism, via the Frankfurt School, and the later waves of feminism and identity politics. Or this crude sexual reductionism may be another example of the broader reductive effect that seems to govern Western thought, in which everything must be reduced to a single explanatory principle or cause. Economics, biology or the gene, patriarchy—God. Who knows?

What is clear beyond a shadow of a doubt, is what the fag interpretation of history does to men and masculinity, and particularly male friendship. The great C.S. Lewis noted this malign tendency in the 1940s, in his essay "Four Types of Love," and offered perhaps the most eloquent rebuttal of it. "Those who cannot conceive of Friendship as a substantive love but only as a disguise or elaboration of *Eros* betray the fact that they have never had a friend." Ouch.

But it's worse than that. Yes, the people who spout this nonsense certainly don't understand what real friendship is, and, yes, they've probably never had a real friend, but they don't want *you* to have a real friend either. Instead, they want men to be isolated from one another, to be thrown back onto other kinds of association that make completely different demands of them and provide a radically different idea of what a man is and should do. For so many men now, the last remaining holdouts of their masculinity are sad little grottoes, their "man caves" filled with toys and trinkets like a young boy's bedroom, where every once in a while they go to hide with the men they call their friends and pretend they're just like the heroes in the films and ball games they watch—until their wives and girlfriends call them back to reality again.

This is what all the snide, dismissive remarks about the trailer for *The End of Men* were really saying, and behind them the broader liberal culture. Don't try to sort out your health and your life, don't try to find real friends who will help you and whom you, in turn, can help. Just carry on as you are: depressed, anxious, and alone, without purpose, shunned and calumnied for being a man and wanting to express your basic masculine instincts. It'll be much easier that way. For the accusers, that is. Because you'll be in hell.

Male Friendship as a Revolutionary Force

WHEN MEN get together, things happen. Most of the time, these are small, pretty normal things. But always there's the potential for something more. It's not an exaggeration to say male friendship is a revolutionary force. Always has been, always will be. History tells us this again and again, from the classical age to the modern. Groups of motivated, well-trained men, bound to one another by shared loyalty and a shared ideal—what could be more formidable—or a more dangerous adversary for corrupt, sclerotic political regimes?

The ancient Greeks understood this well. In Book V of the *Politics*, Aristotle described the best means for tyrants to maintain their rule. Aristotle wasn't *for* tyranny, by the way: He was just writing a description of tyranny in its ideal form, and therefore the ideal means by which tyranny sustained itself, as evidenced by the example of rulers like Periander of Corinth. The tyrant must:

> Lop off those who are too high; he must put to death men of spirit; he must not allow common meals, clubs, education, and the like; he must be upon his guard against anything which is likely to inspire either courage or confidence among his subjects; he must prohibit literary assemblies or other meetings for discussion, and he must take every means to prevent people from knowing one another (for acquaintance begets mutual confidence) . . . [217]

It was an ancient tyrant's duty to ensure that his male citizens didn't get together in pursuit of a better, more righteous way of living, one governed not by fear and suspicion, but positive appreciation of man's true nature. Even then, this duty to prevent "anything which is likely to inspire either courage or confidence among his subjects" could expand to physical exercise, because physical exercise inspired courage and brought men together.

The gymnasia and other institutions of physical cultivation, such as the palaestra (wrestling school), were essential parts of life for Greek men and Greek women. They produced not only physically fit but also virtuous individuals. The gymnasia were bustling with civic life.

> The rooted custom of daily exercise and a bath brought men to the building; and, once there in the company of their fellows, they found that there was no better place for social intercourse, small talk, relaxation, lounging, dissemination of news and views, and serious conversation and discussion. Some of the rooms around the inclosed inner area of a gymnasium were furnished with a few marble seats, like the ornamental ones in our museums today. The Sophists in the late fifth century were the first to use these rooms as lecture halls.[218]

Slavery and Male Friendship Don't Mix

IT'S NO surprise that in ancient Greece, a slaveholding society, slaves were explicitly prohibited from participating in exercises in the gymnasia and the palaestra. If it was right for freemen to cultivate their prowess and virtue—their *thymos*—it was not right for slaves to do so, certainly not during the golden period of the Greek City States.[219] Slaves with *thymos* might get ideas above their station.

Slaves with *thymos* might get ideas above their station—is that *us*? I think the parallels between today's liberalism and yesterday's Classical Greece, and especially the tyrannies, are far from superficial. By telling men they're gay for wanting to work out together, have fun, and break the shackles of modern dependency on junk food, video games and porn, Joy Behar, George Takei, Stephen Colbert and the rest might as well be Periander of Corinth or some other ancient tyrant turning his men against one another and closing the meeting places and gymnasia. The sharp irony of this comparison would, of course, be lost on modern liberals, who only really care about the getting and having of power, but we need to take it seriously if we want to create a society that has a worthy place for men with chests, both in the moral sense C. S. Lewis meant and in the more literal, physical, sense I mean. Liberalism has a tyrannical aspect that is never clearer today than when men start taking control of their lives and cease to be passive consumers.

These people—Behar, Takei, Colbert, et al.—are all leftists, and it might be objected that it isn't liberalism or liberal democracy *per se* that is tyrannical, but leftists and leftism. A quick glance at the last 200 years of history and the struggle of the Cold War might convince you of that. But Fukuyama's analysis makes it quite clear that liberalism by its very nature prevents the full expression and satisfaction of *thymos*. I'll return to this point soon because it's crucial and because it suggests some rather disquieting possibilities about the ultimate solution to the problem of masculine decline today.

Self-Emasculated Democrats

LEFTISTS HAVE now openly embraced emasculation and having low testosterone as part of their identity. This was on absurd display at 2024's Democratic National Convention, when Planned Parenthood took a special mobile clinic to Chicago and offered male convention-goers free vasectomies in a car park near the main venue. Around ten men had themselves sterilized on the first day of the conference. The following day, the mobile clinic offered free abortions. So-called "reproductive rights" were one of the most important issues of the convention, which had a huge inflatable intra-uterine device stationed close to the entrance, just in case attendees were in any doubt.

Vasectomies at the Democratic National Convention, libtard men queueing up to end their lineage for good as a display of political loyalty—it's a bit on the nose, isn't it? Maybe once upon a time, but not today. Literal emasculation now has strong political coding. You may remember there was a significant increase in sterilizations for both sexes, as a result of the Dobbs decision, repealing Roe v. Wade. It was widely reported. The women who had the procedure were protecting themselves from some terrible Handmaiden's Tale-type situation of "forced pregnancy," where Donald Trump, Brett Kavanaugh and Mike Pence tie you down and force you to bring a baby to term, and the men did it out of male-feminist solidarity. "I'm with her," basically—the old Hillary Clinton slogan. According to

John Semley in *The Guardian*, a vasectomy is now "a political gesture . . . a way for men to take a more active stake in big decisions about contraception and reproduction that typically fall to women."[220]

"Shawn," a young man profiled by *The Guardian*, is typical:

> Shawn never really wanted children. A 32-year-old software engineer and amateur weightlifter living in central Florida, he had long contemplated a vasectomy. When he met his fiancée and learned that she also held no grand designs on reproduction, the matter was all but settled. He was, by his estimate, "90 percent certain."

The Supreme Court's recent overturning of Roe v Wade, and the nationwide convulsions over abortion access, was the final push he and his partner needed. When he read that Justice Clarence Thomas mentioned, in his opinion concurring with the controversial ruling, that the court should reconsider access to contraception, Shawn knew he had to move fast.[221]

Shawn sees his vasectomy as "more than just a way of chipping in." "The rolling back of abortion rights has served to strengthen his—and his fiancee's—conviction that procreating at all in the modern U.S. is vaguely immoral." Good for you, Shawn.

Liberal men didn't even wait for the final Dobbs decision to be released. When the draft was leaked in May 2022, daily searches for "Where can I get a vasectomy?" rose 850 percent, says *The Guardian*.

The new generation of hormonal contraceptives—for men, not women—is being advertised in exactly the same manner, as "a way for men to take a more active stake in big decisions about contraception and reproduction that typically fall to women." Here's feminist Jill Filipovic, for *The Guardian*, again:

> Among politically progressive couples especially, it's now standard to expect that a male partner will do his fair share of the household management and childrearing (whether he actually does is a separate question, but the expectation is there). What men generally cannot do, though, is carry pregnancies and birth babies.

And so, for years, women have also been asking when modern medicine will allow men to do their part in at least planning for those babies, and preventing mistimed or unwanted pregnancies. Now that the moment seems near, a male contraceptive will be another test of whether heterosexual men are actually willing to take on the shared responsibilities of adult life, or whether they're satisfied leaving women doing all the work of controlling when and whether to reproduce.[222]

The new male Pill will see the Sexual Revolution, ushered in by its female counterpart, come full circle, at last. Men will finally have the chance to put their money where their partner's mouth is and show they really do believe in equality between the sexes. No more excuses.

The Leftist Hue and Cry for a Male Contraceptive

THE MARKET for male contraceptives has been estimated at $200 billion a year, according to a study published in the journal *Current Obstetrics and Gynecology Reports*.[223] That study assumes a national market of ten million men in the U.S. and a worldwide market of fifty million. A more recent study in the *Journal of Sex Research* claims that between 34 percent and 82.3 percent of men might be willing to use a new male contraceptive, suggesting an international market of hundreds rather than tens of millions.[224]

Very soon, the use of a male contraceptive will become a *sine qua non* for leftist dating. I can confidently predict this. In the same way that during the pandemic vaccination became an essential requirement, in the near future a certain kind of liberal woman will not date a man who doesn't take the lead and use hormonal contraception himself. I can guarantee it. As if dating in the present day could get any worse . . .

Emasculation wasn't just on offer outside the DNC in 2024. Inside the hall, the Party was busy at work selling itself, perhaps for the first time ever in American political history, as the party of low-testosterone men.

What's interesting about this is the shift that's taken place even from 2022, when *The End of Men* was released. In 2022, liberal commentators were keen to mock and throw the fag slur around, but they also disputed the very premises of the documentary. They said testosterone decline either doesn't exist at all—and therefore people who say they care about it are just talking in code about something else, like the loosening grip of "white supremacy" or "the patriarchy"—or they said it simply doesn't matter, because testosterone levels have no political consequences whatsoever. None.

Now, by contrast, we have politicians and commentators telling us testosterone decline does matter, and in fact it's *good* because it makes it more likely that men will accept the future, the future being the nation's first female president.

CNN's Dana Bash announced that Democrats were "trying to put forward male figures—Tim Walz being one of them, Doug Emhoff last night—who can speak to men out there who might not be the testosterone-laden, gun-toting kind of guy who wants to listen to Hulk Hogan and the kind of players that came out of the RNC; but also, in addition, understand that it's okay in 2024 to be a man comfortable in his own skin who supports a woman. And that's something that they're really trying to work on with male voters beyond the base."

Bash and others were appalled by Hulk Hogan's antics at the Republican National Convention, when he ripped his top off during his speech to reveal a Trump-Vance T-shirt and bellowed "LET TRUMPAMANIA RUN WILD, BROTHER!" like it was Madison Square Garden in 1983 and he was about to hit a leg drop on Mr T. The Democrats have no counter to such bonkers, androgenic absurdity. Former pro-wrestler Jesse "the Body" Ventura went on CNN to endorse Kamala Harris, but only because he really, really hates Donald Trump for being a much more successful populist than he is. These days, Jesse's more likely to fall asleep in public than rip his shirt off or rehash his lines from *Predator* about "slack-jawed faggots" and being a "goddamn sexual tyrannosaurus."

Tim Walz and White Minstrelry

RATHER THAN Hulk Hogan, the Democrats offered Tim Walz, with his bizarre posturing, which I referred to somewhere as a "white and white minstrel routine." Walz's whole routine was basically a parody of some liberal theater kid's idea of what a small-town white dude is like, but with a few qualifications. Yes, Walz was a former National Guardsman and a football coach, and he did all the awkward stuff your uncle does when he's had a little bit too much eggnog at

Christmas, like pogoing to John Mellencamp and high-fiving everyone in sight, but Walz was also a man who says the kind of banal things that would be right at home on a childless cat lady's Instagram page. Things like, "Surround yourself with smart women and listen to them, and you'll do just fine" (he actually said that). Tim Walz offers America "tonic masculinity, the antidote to toxic masculinity," *Axios* said.[225]

If modern leftism is increasingly inclined toward emasculation, we have every reason to believe the biological assault on masculinity will create more leftists. This is a self-perpetuating problem, then, a vicious cycle: More men become leftists, and leftist governments make social conditions even less propitious for traditional masculinity—and so on. Downwards we go. This has been an implicit part of the narrative so far, but it's time I made it explicit.

We're a long way away from a proper hormonal theory of politics, one that fully acknowledges first, the role hormones play in political decision-making and affiliation and second, that there may be something distinct about the modern hormonal environment that explains or is necessary to understand the modern political environment as well.

The Left and Learned Helplessness

THE LATE Dr. Ray Peat, with his theory of bioenergetics, drew attention to the pervasive modern condition of "learned helplessness"—in which animals and humans are conditioned to failure and therefore become apathetic, docile and easier to govern—and linked it to chronic exposure to estrogenic substances, as well as chronic stress more broadly.[226] On this view, the techniques of mass control used by modern governments, which were on such prominent display during the pandemic, would not be possible without a biological organism that is already conditioned to be in a state of permanent stress and therefore resigned to having little or no say in its own fate. Totalitarianism is at work both outside and inside the human body to a degree that not even as pessimistic a writer as Solzhenitsyn could have known.

When it comes to testosterone and leftism, there's plenty of very suggestive evidence, most of it indirect—especially studies that link low testosterone to traits we would associate with leftism, and higher testosterone to right-wing traits—but also some more direct evidence explicitly linking the two. An unpublished study, for example, shows that "testosterone administration induces a red shift in Democrats." Here's a summary of the study's findings by the author, Paul Zak:

> We tested the fixity of political preferences of 136 healthy males during the 2011 U.S. presidential election season by administering synthetic testosterone or placebo to participants who had identified the strength of their political affiliation. Before the testosterone treatment, we found that weakly affiliated Democrats had 19 percent higher basal testosterone than those who identified strongly with the party (p=0.015). When weakly affiliated Democrats received additional testosterone, the strength of their party fell by 12 percent (p=.01) and they reported 45 percent warmer feelings towards Republican candidates for president (p < 0.001). Our results demonstrate that testosterone induces a "red shift" among weakly-affiliated Democrats. This effect was associated with improved mood. No effects were found of testosterone administration for strongly affiliated Democrats or strong or weak Republicans. Our findings provide evidence that neuroactive hormones affect political preferences.[227]

So, if you give "weakly affiliated" Democrats a dose of testosterone, they suddenly start to warm to Mitt Romney. That's no mean feat. It's interesting that the hormone only seems to work on Democrats who are closer to the center of the political spectrum. If I were to conduct a follow-on study, I'd experiment with dosages and see if a higher dose was able to work on strongly affiliated Democrats, or whether no amount of testosterone could shake them out of their allegiance. A giga-dose just might work but remember: I'm not claiming that testosterone is *all* that determines politics, only that it's an important factor that's yet to be fully appreciated.

Testosterone and Partisan Behavior

WHAT'S INTERESTING about this research, too, is that the researcher found an association with improved mood, which points to the broader benefits of having higher testosterone and suggests how they might contribute to a more right-wing outlook. It's also been shown that leftists are more mentally ill than right-wingers;[228] that they're less happy;[229] that they're more neurotic and emotionally unstable[230]—all mood traits that could be directly associated with testosterone levels in men.

Indeed, there are plenty of other studies that suggest very clearly, but in a less direct way, that testosterone levels are likely to have aggregate effects on political behavior. If there's one fundamental difference between right and left, it concerns hierarchy and the attitude to it. In basic terms, you could say hierarchy—inequality, for example—is proper and essential to right-wingers, while leftists in their various iterations, from communists to anarchists to socialists and even plain old libtards, do as much as they can to eliminate it wherever they find it. That's a statement, I think, we can all agree on. A number of studies show that testosterone significantly modulates the male attitude to hierarchy in ways that might determine whether a man tends right or left.

Take this study, for example: "Testosterone administration modulates inequality aversion in healthy males: evidence from computational modeling."[231] Young men were given either a dose of testosterone gel or a placebo. Three hours later, they were asked to play a game in which they had to allocate resources anonymously in either a "fair" or "unfair" manner. "Participants were either in a position of advantageous inequality (i.e., endowed with more than others) or disadvantageous inequality (i.e., endowed with less than others)." The men who received the testosterone boost "showed significantly reduced aversion to advantageous inequality but enhanced aversion to disadvantageous inequality." Basically, the men with higher T were happier to possess more than the others—hierarchy and inequality, the cornerstone of the right-wing worldview, were not a problem to them.

What's interesting about this study isn't just the results; it's the way they're presented. Here's the final conclusion in the paper's abstract: "These findings suggest that testosterone facilitates decisions that prioritize selfish economic motives over fairness concerns, which in turn may boost status-enhancing behaviors." So attitude to hierarchy is collapsed into "selfish economic motives" and "status-enhancing behaviors." It's always worth remembering that science itself, and especially a discipline like social psychology, is not a neutral frame. All sorts of values and social judgments are baked into modern science in the West, as surely as they were baked into science in the communist Eastern Bloc, or scientific inquiry wherever it has been practiced. To return to the language of Francis Fukuyama and the ancient Greeks, we could say that, to a bunch of *isothymic* social psychologists, born and raised in an *isothymic* system, a display of *megalothymia* can only be coded negatively, as a deviation from and a threat to the healthy social norm, which is equality.

Testosterone and the Male Warrior

TESTOSTERONE MODULATES hierarchical behavior in more complicated ways than are dreamed of by the authors of "Testosterone Administration Modulates Inequality Aversion in Healthy Males: Evidence from Computational Modeling." Far from merely making men want to excel over everyone else and have the most resources and status, studies suggest testosterone administration affects men differently according to their place within a hierarchy. Consider this study: "Testosterone promotes either dominance or submissiveness in the Ultimatum Game depending on players' social rank."[232] Japanese researchers looked at the testosterone levels of players in a university rugby team—"where a strong seniority norm maintains hierarchical relationships"—and assessed their behavior in an ultimatum game, where two players offered each other rewards. The results showed that testosterone levels altered the players' behavior according to their status within the team's hierarchy. Higher status players with higher testosterone were less likely to acquiesce to ultimatums, whereas lower status players with higher testosterone were more likely to. So this suggests testosterone levels are essential to the maintenance of proper hierarchy at every level. It's not just that testosterone makes hierarchy seem more natural: it also makes men fit into it better.

Here's a second clear way in which testosterone promotes what we might call archetypal right-wing attitudes and behavior: parochial altruism. Parochial altruism, the preference for one's own in-group at the expense of others, separates right- and left-wingers pretty neatly, and lies at the root of differences on a range of issues from welfare to immigration. A person with higher levels of parochial altruism would be more likely to support immigration restriction, for example, to protect what they perceive as their own people, than somebody with low parochial altruism, who would probably plant a flag on their front lawn saying "In this house we believe: Diversity is our strength."

There are many studies that show a clear link between testosterone levels and parochial altruism. In a classic prisoner's dilemma game—where two people can either cooperate for mutual gain or betray each other for their own benefit—male soccer fans with high testosterone were more likely to cooperate with other male soccer fans if they supported the same team.[233] They were also more likely to betray partners who supported a different team. This demonstrates one way in which the "testosterone equals aggression" thesis is clearly wrong. What matters is whether you're in the in-group or the out-group. If you're in the in-group, you get altruistic behavior from men with higher testosterone. But if you're in the out-group, you don't.

Evolutionary psychologists have put forward what they call the "male warrior hypothesis" to explain this, claiming that sex-specific pressures would have favored cooperation among men in smaller tribal groups and hostility to outsiders:

> Archaeological and comparative evidence indicates that inter-group conflict has been present since the dawn of our lineage. Anthropological studies of tribal societies in the 20th and 21st centuries have shed light on the benefits of inter-group conflict for males, shaped by sexual selection to compete through

physical aggression. The male warrior hypothesis argues that "humans, particularly men, may possess psychological mechanisms enabling them to form coalitions capable of planning, initiating and executing acts of aggression on members of outgroups, with the ultimate goal of acquiring or protecting reproductive resources . . ."

The male warrior hypothesis is a sex-specific proposal primarily supported theoretically by the greater degree of variance among men than among women in terms of reproductive success and the lower level of obligatory parental investment by men. These two factors have enhanced intrasexual competition in men, thus favoring sexual dimorphism in size and strength, accompanied by a significant sex-based difference in physical aggressiveness. In this sense, men have enormous incentives to form coalitions to be involved in intergroup contests because of the benefits associated with winning these contests, even if the costs of losing the contest could be devastating. Therefore, in contrast to women, men can exacerbate intra-group cooperation and intergroup aggression in the context of an intergroup threat, the most important factor triggering these behaviors being the incentives to monopolize resources.[234]

Whatever the reasons for the emergence of this association, testosterone appears to be essential to the maintenance of group boundaries, favoring cohesion among the in-group and encouraging hostility to be directed outwards beyond the tribe, village, nation—whatever.

Testosterone, Fear, Loathing, and Politics

I'D ARGUE that these two aspects of personality and behavior—"inequality aversion" and "parochial altruism"—go a long way towards distinguishing the biological basis of archetypal left- and right-wing positions. There's more research, too, that could help to build the case for testosterone as a key variable in political allegiance, and help us understand why the collapse of male testosterone levels matters specifically as a political event.

There are studies of the brain's amygdala region, which is involved in threat-perception. Researchers have demonstrated that leftists have smaller amygdalas, the implication being that altered threat-perception might be a key difference between left- and right-wing perspectives.[235] It's not hard to see how altered threat perception might underlie attitudes towards altruism and everything that that entails, with a keener sense of threat driving more recognizably right-wing attitudes (e.g. tightly controlled borders, reduced welfare, laws against vagrancy and homelessness, and so on).

We also know that testosterone modulates the function of the amygdala. One study showed, for example, that the amygdala works harder in socially threatening situations when a person has more testosterone.[236] It's widely known that amygdala responses to images of angry faces are stronger in people who have been given a dose of testosterone.

A proper hormonal theory of politics is some way off. There's more work to be done on the specific mechanisms of testosterone's action on attitudes and behavior more generally, and tying hormonal levels to political orientation remains a controversial approach. The re-election of Donald Trump may make it easier for such research to take place in the U.S., or it could have the opposite effect—we'll see.

And it's not just men we should be thinking about either. We have good reason to believe that the estrogenicity of the modern world is affecting women's political behavior in similar ways. Indeed, the main thrust of modern leftism is coming from women now, and the changing hormonal environment is likely a factor. For example, massive use of hormonal contraception may be altering women's political behavior on a large scale. It's reckoned that 150 million women worldwide use hormonal birth control today.

The Pill Shrinks the Brain

A RECENT study showed hormonal birth control appears to shrink a key region of the brain, the ventromedial prefrontal cortex, which is involved in fear processing and emotional control.[237] It was already known that hormonal birth control is associated with morphological changes to the brain, but this recent study is the most detailed and most worrying yet. We already had direct and indirect evidence for this, like the fact that teenagers who use hormonal contraception and then stop face a lifetime increased risk of depression, whereas the depression risk for adult women who discontinue use returns back to the average—suggesting hormonal contraception causes permanent structural changes to the developing teenage brain.[238]

For the brain-shrinking study, the researchers recruited a number of different groups of women and men. These included women who were using hormonal contraceptives at the time of the study, women who had used them in the past, women who had never used any, and men, as a control. The researchers used MRI imaging to measure regions of the brain and investigate whether hormonal contraceptives were linked with differences in the structure of the brain, and whether there might be sex-based differences.

The ventromedial prefrontal cortex in women who were currently using hormonal contraceptives was significantly thinner compared to men. Interestingly, this reduced thickness was not observed in women who had discontinued use of hormonal contraceptives in the past, which suggests the structural changes—and any behavioral deficits—are reversible if use of the drugs ceases. The researchers behind the study are now exploring whether age of first use and length of use are factors. As I noted above, use of hormonal contraception as a teenager has different, permanent, effects on depression risk from use as a fully grown adult.

Changes to key areas of the brain as a result of exposure to artificial hormones, especially areas involved in emotional regulation, are bound to have knock-on effects at the aggregate level, beyond personal relationships and the strain put on them by use of hormonal contraceptives. Disinhibition of millions of women—the dysregulation of fear, in particular—could be one reason, or at least a contributing factor, for the profound gender split that has been noticed in countries across the Developed World, with women becoming unmoored from men and drifting further and further leftward.[239]

We like to imagine that our opponents—the people who vote for open borders and mass immigration and the mutilation of children and the early release of violent criminals—have shrunken brains, but it may actually be true, at least in the case of our female opponents. And the Pill may be the reason, or at least part of it.

As soon as the brain-shrinking study came out, the authors cautioned against drawing conclusions about large-scale behavior, but frankly that's unavoidable. The potential implications are obvious, even if further research needs to be done. Their caution was largely a reflection of the sensitivity of the topic of women's reproductive rights, especially in the aftermath of the Dobbs decision, and the enormous money involved in the sale of hormonal birth control.

Viral social-media campaigns to get women to give up birth control because of the side effects, such as weight gain and mood changes, meet with furious reaction and cries of "disinformation" from the mainstream media.

You see that sensitivity on display even in a book as straightforwardly damning as Sarah Hill's *This Is Your Brain on Birth Control*, which contains a litany of studies about the mental, emotional and physical harms hormonal birth control causes. Hill feels compelled to engage in constant hedging—"I'm not saying don't take birth control," "Of course it's up to you to decide whether you stop taking it"—even as she describes terrifying side effect after terrifying side effect. Part of this, no doubt, is the elevation of "personal choice" as the highest of all values that modern women can pursue, so that any kind of barrier to unfettered choice, including well-meaning advice and wisdom gained from personal experience—by women!—is seen as an unwelcome, even immoral, intrusion.

As Voltaire famously didn't say (but somebody did), "To learn who rules over you, simply find out who you are not allowed to criticize." Birth control, it seems, rules over women today.

CHAPTER 7

Outroduction

"The war against war is going to be no holiday excursion or camping party. The military feelings are too deeply grounded to abdicate their place among our ideals until better substitutes are offered than the glory and shame that come to nations as well as to individuals from the ups and downs of politics and the vicissitudes of trade."

—WILLIAM JAMES, *The Moral Equivalent of War*

"Pain is one of the keys to unlock man's innermost being as well as the world. Whenever one approaches the points where man proves himself to be equal to or superior to pain, one gains access to the sources of his power and the secret behind his dominion. Tell me your relation to pain, and I will tell you who you are!"

—ERNST JÜNGER, *On Pain*

— ♦♦♦ —

The Last Men—or Something Worse?

THE AMERICAN philosopher William James, like Francis Fukuyama, was concerned by modern life and its effects on masculinity.

James was a self-confessed pacifist and a socialist, but he recognized that the martial virtues, cultivated and discharged through warfare, were essential to social cohesion and a national sense of purpose. Without them, a nation could only weaken and, almost inevitably, be conquered by a more vigorous nation that had not forgotten the old ways of war. And even if it weren't conquered, a nation that couldn't harness the warlike spirit would fall into lassitude, aimlessness, and decay.

In his 1910 essay, "The Moral Equivalent of War," James tried to present an alternative to war, to reverse this general decline. War without war, if you will. He wanted the social benefits, but not the tremendous suffering and pointless destruction that worked against the general trend towards progress and social improvement he so cherished.

James believed that the retreat from warfare was making society weak, not least of all because warlikeness, "pugnacity," is inborn in man, as a result of our long evolution and the survival of the fittest:

Such was the gory nurse that trained societies to cohesiveness. We inherit the warlike type; and for most of the capacities of heroism that the human race is full of we have to thank this cruel history. Dead men tell no tales, and if there were any tribes of other type than this they have left no survivors. Our ancestors have bred pugnacity into our bone and marrow, and thousands of years of peace won't breed it out of us. The popular imagination fairly fattens on the thought of wars. Let public opinion once reach a certain fighting pitch, and no ruler can withstand it.[240]

For the longest period of time, even peace itself has been a preparation for war, and therefore a part of it. "The battles are only a sort of public verification of the mastery gained during the 'peace' interval," James adds.

What James proposes can be described as a "war against nature," rather than a war against our fellow man. By enlisting young men in a struggle against nature, through a kind of quasi-conscription, "the military ideals of hardihood and discipline would be wrought into the growing fiber of the people; no one would remain blind as the luxurious classes now are blind, to man's relations to the globe he lives on, and to the permanently sour and hard foundation of his higher life":

To coal and iron mines, to freight trains, to fishing fleets in December, to dish-washing, clothes-washing, and window-washing, to road-building and tunnel-making, to foundries and stoke-holes, and to the frames of sky-scrapers, would our gilded youths be drafted off, according to their choice, to get the childishness knocked out of them, and to come back into society with healthier sympathies and soberer ideas. They would have paid their blood-tax, done their own part in the immemorial human warfare against nature; they would tread the earth more proudly, the women would value them more highly, they would be better fathers and teachers of the next generation.[241]

The William James Prescription for Fukuyama's Pessimism

IN MANY ways, what James is saying is simply a paraphrase of Fukuyama's thesis about the fate of *thymos*, and *megalothymia* in particular, in the modern world. In both cases, fundamental aspects of masculine behavior no longer have an outlet, with potentially dire social effects.

The difference between the two accounts is that James offers a prescriptive solution. Fukuyama, by contrast, simply offers an observation, in line with what Freud says in *Civilization and Its Discontents*: undischarged instincts and urges, on a large enough scale, imperil society and make it ripe for dissolution.[242] Freud, at least, believed that such a society, when it repressed man's instincts, deserved reaction and revolution. If a society's rulers created a system that prevented their people from leading a satisfying life, it was only right that the ordinary people should rise up and overthrow them in the name of a system that would be satisfying.

Fukuyama's account is more pessimistic, without prescription. With liberalism as the end stage of political development, there isn't really any room for fundamental change. This is it. There's nothing more.

As I noted right at the beginning of the book, Fukuyama suggests the post-1989 future will be marked by what he calls "immense wars of the spirit;" "for the absence of regular and constructive outlets for *megalothymia* may sim-

ply lead to its later resurgence in an extreme and patho-
logical form":

> How long *megalothymia* will be satisfied with metaphorical
> wars and symbolic victories is an open question. One sus-
> pects that some people will not be satisfied until they prove
> themselves by that very act that constituted their humanness
> at the beginning of history: they will want to risk their lives
> in a violent battle, and thereby prove beyond any shadow of
> a doubt to themselves and to their fellows that they are free.
> They will deliberately seek discomfort and sacrifice, because
> the pain will be the only way they have of proving defini-
> tively that they can *think well of themselves*, that they remain
> *human beings*.[243]

Fukuyama—"metaphorical wars and symbolic victories"—could be gesturing towards William James here and
his "war with nature." He mentions Donald Trump, the
mountain-climber Reinhold Meissner, and George Bush as
examples of men who achieve a high degree of *megalothymic* satisfaction through great endeavors and overweening
ambition, but then adds that even "the causes they serve are
not the most serious or the most just." Ted Kaczynski, a.k.a.
"The Unabomber," noted with great perspicacity the failure
of all so-called "surrogate activities" to replicate the satisfaction of the real thing. For Kaczynski, this was one of the
fundamental reasons why industrial society, which offers us
only a surrogate existence, must end.

In many ways, Fukuyama has been proven right. What,
for example, is radical Islam and the ISIS caliphate if not the
reassertion of *megalothymia*, religiously tinged of course, in
the face of the spread of Western liberal institutions across
the Middle East?

At the same time, as he looked at the West itself, Fukuyama doubted that there could be a reassertion on a widespread level of man's desire for distinction over his fellow man:

> Looking around contemporary America, it does not strike me that we face the problem of an excess of *megalothymia*. Those earnest young people trooping off to law and business school, who anxiously fill out their resumés in hope of maintaining the lifestyles to which they believe themselves entitled, seem to be much more in danger of becoming last men, rather than reviving the passions of the first man. For them, the liberal project of filling one's life with material acquisitions and safe, sanctioned ambitions appears to have worked all too well. It is hard to detect great, unfulfilled longings or irrational passions lurking just beneath the surface of the average first-year law student.[244]

Beyond the Last Men?

THAT MAY be so, especially on the basis of what I've said throughout this book about the parallel biological decline of *thymos*. Under the combined assault of endocrine-disrupting chemicals, poor diet, and maladaptive lifestyles, male potency faces an existential challenge. Rather than occupying a position where masculinity, driven by testosterone, finds itself frustrated by the constraints of liberal democracy, we now face the total undoing of masculinity and, indeed, gender itself. Far from being the Last Men, we could end up as something even worse than that.

I've shown you ways to salvage your health and regain your biological inheritance, from exercising and fixing your sleep to filtering your water and ditching processed foods.

In the U.S., at least, there are finally the beginnings of a society-wide movement for health, with Robert F. Kennedy Jr. at its head. It will take many years—far longer than a single presidential term—to fix America's health crisis, which has been seventy or more years, probably a century, in the making.

Only then, if we do, will we even have to face the questions about the decline of *thymos* raised by Fukuyama in his most famous book. Only then will it be up to us to decide whether we really are the Last Men he describes—or whether a different kind of existence, and a different kind of history, is still within our grasp.

Ten Steps to Raw Egg Nationalism

– ♦♦♦ –

Increase Your Testosterone, Reawaken Your Health and Conquer Life

A LTHOUGH THIS list of points is aimed at men, every single one of these recommendations would benefit women just as much.

1. Banish Plastic from Your Life

PLASTIC IS one of the principal sources of exposure to harmful endocrine-disruptors. Do everything you can to reduce your reliance on plastic in any form, even if you can't totally eliminate it from your life (you can't).

Here are some easy things you can do to begin with:

+ Don't drink from plastic bottles.

+ Don't heat food in plastic in the microwave.

+ Don't store food in plastic.

+ Stop buying processed food. (See next step.)

+ Replace your plastic chopping board with a wooden one.

Banishing plastic also means thinking about the things you wear and your furnishings, many of which will be made of synthetic fibres and shed microplastics in great quantity around your home. Prefer natural fibres to synthetic, and vacuum your house regularly to prevent microplastics accruing in dust. This is especially important if you have a young child, because they'll be crawling around close to the floor, doing a very lifelike impression of a hoover. If you have a young child, you should also prevent them from playing with plastic toys or putting plastic of any kind in their mouth: not just toys but also utensils and things like sippy cups and bottles.

2. Get Serious in the Kitchen

LEARNING HOW to cook is one of the most powerful interventions you can make to regain control of your health. At a stroke, you no longer have to rely on other people to prepare your food for you. You don't need to buy processed food anymore or rely on calorie- and chemical-laden takeaway food.

Getting serious in the kitchen also means getting rid of cookware that could be harming your health. Pots and pans with non-stick coatings leach harmful chemicals into your food and, as the coating degrades over time, millions of microplastic particles. Copper, ceramic or stainless steel cookware is much better. By learning to cook properly and control the temperature in the pan, you won't need a special Teflon coating to prevent your steak or omelette from getting stuck.

3. Eat Like Your Ancestors: Animal-Based Is Best

AS WESTON Price showed, diets rooted in nutrient-dense animal foods produce the healthiest, most beautiful people.

This is how our ancestors ate for the longest period of time, and it's how you should eat too if you want to have optimal health and boost your body's flagging hormones. Make animal foods—lean meat, fatty cuts, organ meat, dairy, eggs, fish and shellfish—the main focus of your meals, and try to make sure you get the best you can. The healthier and happier the animal, the more nutritious the food it produces—and the better you can feel about eating it.

4. Filter Your Water

TAP WATER is invariably contaminated with harmful chemicals, some of which, like fluoride, may even be added deliberately by your local municipality. Invest in a carbon filter and reverse-osmosis system to purify your water as much as possible. Think of a crystal-clear mountain stream and make that your goal.

5. Purge Your Home of Harmful Chemicals

MOST OF your exposure to harmful chemicals takes place in the ordinary course of your daily life, in mundane activities like eating, drinking, washing and using personal-care products and even working in the garden. You're topping up your levels of harmful chemicals every day by using the same products that contain the same harmful chemicals. The way to break this cycle is to stop using these products altogether, or find replacements that contain fewer or no harmful chemicals.

Soaps, lotions, fragrances, deodorants, cosmetics and air fresheners all contain endocrine-disrupting chemicals. So do laundry detergents. If you're a keen gardener, get rid of artificial pesticides and herbicides and learn permaculture methods to keep on top of weeds and maximise your yields.

6. Lose Weight

FAT MASS is inversely related to testosterone levels: the more fat you have, the lower your testosterone is likely to be. Excess fat is also associated with reduced fertility and increased risk for more or less every chronic disease there is.

Pay heed to the basic principles of thermodynamics and make sure your body is burning more energy than it's taking in. Diet alone can take you far with weight loss, but it's much better—and more fun—if you get moving as well.

If you're starting a programme of exercise for the first time, take it slow. Maybe just start going for walks. Build in small increments, and before you know it you won't believe how far you've come.

Monitor your progress and keep a journal to ensure you remain accountable.

7. Build Muscle

BUILDING MUSCLE is one of the best ways to increase your testosterone levels as a man. It's also the best "hedge" against weight-gain in the long term, ensuring your body's metabolic furnace is burning hot, even if you stop exercising. Building muscle means lifting weights. If you've never lifted before, heed my advice with the previous recommendation: take it slow and build in small increments. Monitor your progress.

8. Detoxify by Sweating

ANOTHER BENEFIT of exercise is that sweating helps detoxify your body. Harmful chemicals stored in your body's fat stores are mobilised and make their way to the skin, where they pass into the sweat and out of the body. You can also use the sauna to purge your body of harmful chemicals too, but don't do it too regularly as a man: the heat can affect testicular function.

9. Go to Sleep!

PROPER SLEEP is vital to good health, across the board. As I noted in the main text, an older man can double his testosterone simply by doubling his nightly sleep from four to eight hours. There's an epidemic of sleeplessness today, but sleep is one of the last things people think to improve.

Try to establish a regular pattern for sleeping, following the earth's natural diurnal rhythms (i.e. when the sun rises and sets). Modify your home environment to reflect these rhythms. Lower the lights in the evening, reduce the warmth in the house—or take a warm shower or bath to reduce your core body temperature—and stop using electronic devices well before you intend to go to bed. The blue light emitted from electronic devices tricks your body into thinking it's still daytime. Sleep preparations like these are called "sleep hygiene," and there are a variety of other things you can do to improve it as well.

10. Don't Be Fooled by Quick Fixes

YOU MAY be one of the unlucky men who has a congenital testosterone problem, in which case testosterone-replacement therapy is almost certainly the answer for you. But it's likely that you don't, so before you go to your doctor for a prescription, try optimising your health in the ways I've listed above. That should be enough to transform your health, and you'll feel even better about yourself, and be better equipped to deal with life, because you've done it all on your own.

Also remember: no medical treatment is without side effects: testosterone-replacement therapy is no different. If you start on it, you may have to remain on it for the rest of your life.

Beware too the new GLP-1-receptor-agonist drugs like Ozempic. Some people probably can't lose weight without them—they're simply too fat—but that's unlikely to be you. You can lose weight, with application, and you'll only benefit, as a whole person, from doing so. Again, there are also side effects. With these new weight-loss drugs, these extend up to and include death, but they're mainly things like stomach paralysis, uncontrollable diarrhea and, in the long term, thyroid cancer. Not nice, especially when the risk isn't even necessary to begin with.

NOTES

1   Richard V. Reeves, *Of Boys and Men: Why the Modern Male is Struggling, Why it Matters, and What to Do About It.* Washington, D.C: Brookings Institution Press, 2022.

2   Francis Fukuyama, *The End of History and the Last Man.* New York: Free Press, 2006.

3   *The End of Men.* Directed by Scooter Downey and Tucker Carlson. Presented by Tucker Carlson. Fox Nation, 2022, streaming video, https://nation.foxnews.com/watch/tucker-carlson-originals-the-end-of-men/.

4   Fukuyama, "*The End of History*," The National Interest 16 (1989), 4.

5   Fukuyama, *The End of History and the Last Man* (2012), p. 301.

6   Fukuyama, *The End of History and the Last Man*, p. 301.

7   Fukuyama, *The End of History and the Last Man*, p. 163.

8   Fukuyama, *The End of History and the Last Man*, p. 165.

9   Michel Houellebecq, *Plateforme. Paris: Flammarion*, 2001.

10 Weston A. Price, *Nutrition and Physical Degeneration: A Comparison of Primitive and Modern Diets and Their Effects.* Santa Monica, Price-Pottenger Foundation, 1970.

11 Cawley et al., "Direct Medical Costs of Obesity in the United States and the Most Populous States," *Journal of Managed Care and Specialty Pharmacy* 27:3 (2021), doi.org/10.18553/jmcp.2021.20410.

12 https://www.pewresearch.org/short-reads/2023/02/08/for-valentines-day-5-facts-about-single-americans/.

13   "The Share of Americans Not Having Sex Has Reached a Record High," *The Washington Post*, https://www.washingtonpost.com/business/2019/03/29/share-americans-not-having-sex-has-reached-record-high/.

14   Reeves, *Of Boys and Men*, p. 89.

15   Reeves, *Of Boys and Men*, p. xi.

16   Bronze Age Pervert, *Bronze Age Mindset: An Exhortation*. Independently published 2018.

17   O'Donnell et al., "The Health of Normally Aging Men: The Massachusetts Male Aging Study (1987-2004)," *Experimental Gerontology* 39 (2004), https://doi.org/10.1016/j.exger.2004.03.023.

18   https://academic.oup.com/jcem/article/92/1/196/2598434.

19   Travison et al., "A Population-level Decline in Serum Testosterone Levels in American Men," *The Journal of Endocrinology and Metabolism* 92:1 (2007), https://doi.org/10.1210/jc.2006-1375.

20   Travison et al.

21   Travison et al.

22   Perheentupa et al., "A Cohort Effect on Serum Testosterone Levels in Finnish Men," *European Journal of Endocrinology* 168:2 (2013), http://dx.doi.org/10.1530/EJE-12-0288.

23   Andersson et al., "Secular Decline in Male Testosterone and Sex Hormone Binding Globulin Serum Levels in Danish Population Surveys," *The Journal of Clinical Endocrinology and Metabolism* 92:12 (2007), https://doi.org/10.1210/jc.2006-2633.

24   Lokeshwar et al., "Decline in Serum Testosterone Levels among Adolescent and Young Adult Men in the USA," *European Urology Focus* 7:4 (2021), https://doi.org/10.1016/j.euf.2020.02.006.

25   Chodick et al., "Secular Trends in Testosterone- Findings from a Large State-mandate Care Provider," *Reproductive Biology and Endocrinology* 18 (2020), https://doi.org/10.1186/s12958-020-00575-2.

26   Cieri et al., "Craniofacial Feminization, Social Tolerance, and the Origins of Behavioral Modernity," *Current Anthropology* 55:4 (2014), https://doi.org/10.1086/677209.

27   If you're interested in this subject, read Hammes and Levin, "Impact of Estrogens in Males and Androgens in Females," *The Journal of Clinical Investigation* 129:5 (2019), doi.org/10.1172/JCI125755.

28   Simon et al., "Increased Aggressive Behavior and Decreased Affiliative Behavior in Adult Male Monkeys after Long-term Consumption of Diets

Rich in Soy Protein and Isoflavones," *Hormones and Behavior* 45:4 (2004), https://doi.org/10.1016/j.yhbeh.2003.12.005.

29   Simon et al., "Increased Aggressive Behavior and Decreased Affiliative Behavior in Adult Male Monkeys after Long-term Consumption of Diets Rich in Soy Protein and Isoflavones."

30   Rostom et al., "History of Testosterone Therapy through the Ages," *International Journal of Impotence Research* 34 (2022), doi.org/10 .1038/s41443-021-00493-w.

31   Sagoe et al., "The Global Epidemiology of Anabolic-androgenic Steroid Use: A Meta-analysis and Meta-regression Analysis," *Annals of Epidemiology* 24:5 (2014), doi.org/10.1016/j.annepidem.2014.01.009.

32   Sagoe at al., "Attitudes towards Use of Anabolic-androgenic Steroids among Ghanaian High School Students," *International Journal of Drug Policy* 26:2 (2015), https://doi.org/10.1016/j.drugpo.2014.10.004.

33   Belcastro et al., "Hyperostosis frontalis interna (HFI) and castration: the case of the famous singer Farinelli (1705–1782)," *Journal of Anatomy* 219:5 (2011), https://doi.org/10.1111/j.1469-7580.2011.01413.x.

34   Rostom et al., "History of Testosterone Therapy through the Ages," *International Journal of Impotence Research* 34 (2022), doi.org/10 .1038/s41443-021-00493-w.

35   Liao et al., "Testosterone Administration Modulates Inequality Aversion in Healthy Males: Evidence from Computational Modeling," *Psychoneuroendocrinology* 155: 106321 (2023), https://doi.org/10 .1016/j.psyneuen.2023.106321.

36   Kelly et al., "Beyond Sex and Aggression: Testosterone Rapidly Matches Behavioral Responses to Social Context and Tries to Predict the Future," *Proceedings of the Royal Society B: Biological Sciences* 289: 1976 (2022), https://doi.org/10.1098/rspb.2022.0453.

37   Jaeggi et al., "Salivary Oxytocin Increases Concurrently with Testosterone and Time Away from Home among Returning Tsimane' Hunters," *Biology Letters* 11: 3 (2015), https://doi.org/10.1098/rsbl.2015.0058.

38   paulbartmallcop1996. "Want to Share My Story." r/LowT Reddit, 2019. https://www.reddit.com/r/LowT/comments/fw1oud/wanted to share_ my_story/.

39   The complete thread can be found here: https://www.reddit.com/r/LowT/.

40   Anaissie et al., "Testosterone Deficiency in Adults and Corresponding Treatment Patterns across the Globe," *Translational Andrology and Urology* 6:2 (2017), https://doi.org/10.21037/tau.2016.11.16.

41   "Why Won't 541,000 Young Japanese Leave the House?" *CNN* https:// edition.cnn.com/2016/09/11/asia/japanese-millennials-hikikomori- social-recluse/index.html.

42   "Nonprofits in Japan Help 'Shut-ins' Get Out in the Open," *The Japan Times,* https://www.japantimes.co.jp/news/2011/10/09/national/media-national/nonprofits-in-japan-help-shut-ins-get-out-into-the-open/.

43   "Japan's 'Hikikomori' Phenomenon Could Top 10 Million," *Nippon* (2019), https://www.nippon.com/en/japan-topics/c05008/japan%E2%80%99s-hikikomori-population-could-top-10-million.html.

44   See, for example, Teo and Gaw, "Hikikomori, A Japanese Culture-Bound Syndrome of Social Withdrawal? A Proposal for DSM-V," *The Journal of Nervous and Mental Disease* 198:6 (2010), doi.org/10.1097/NMD.0b013e3181e086b1.

45   Hayashi et al., "Social Withdrawal and Testosterone Levels in Early Adolescent Boys," *Pyschoneuroendocrinology* 116 (2020), https://doi.org/10.1016/j.psyneuen.2020.104596.

46   Teo and Gaw, "Hikikomori, A Japanese Culture-Bound Syndrome of Social Withdrawal? A Proposal for DSM-V."

47   For Korea: "Social Isolation Takes a Toll on a Rising Number of South Korea's Young Adults," https://www.npr.org/2024/02/11/1229437757/social-isolation-south-korea. On unemployed young men in America, N. Eberstadt, *Men Without Work: Post Pandemic Edition* (2022).

48   C. S. Lewis, "The Abolition of Man" in *The Abolition of Man, or, Reflections on Education with Special Reference to the Teaching of English in the Upper Forms of Schools.* New York: Simon & Schuster, 1996, p. 408.

49   Ioannis N. Tsoulogiannis and Demetrios A. Spandidos, "Endocrinology in Ancient Sparta," *Hormones vol. 6:1,* Athens, Greece: 2007, p. 80–82.

50   Tsoulogiannis and Spandidos, "Endocrinology in Ancient Sparta," *Hormones.*

51   See Barry Cunliffe, *The Scythians: Nomad Warriors of the Steppe.* Oxford University Press, 2019, pp. 199–201.

52   Pseudo-Hippocrates from Cunliffe, *The Scythians: Nomad Warriors of the Steppe,* 199-201.

53   Derek Hawkins, "Amazons Were Long Considered Myth. These Discoveries Show Warrior Women Were Real," *The Washington Post (2019).* https://www.washingtonpost.com/science/2019/12/31/amazons-were-long-considered-myth-these-discoveries-show-warrior-women-were-real/.

54   "Association between Obesity and Sperm Quality," *Andrologia* (2018) https://doi.org/10.1111/and.12888.

55   "Obesity as Disruptor of the [sic] Female Fertility," *Reproductive Biology and Endocrinology* (2018) https://doi.org/10.1186/s12958-018-0336-z.

56   "Effect of Posture and Clothing on Scrotal Temperature in Fertile Men," *Journal of Andrology* (2007), https://doi.org/10.2164/jandrol.106.000646.

57   "Type of Underwear Worn and Markers of Testicular Function among Men Attending a Fertility Center," *Human Reproduction* (2018) https://doi.org/10.1093/humrep/dey259; "Skinny Jeans Cause Health Problems for Men," *Medical News Today* https://www.medicalnewstoday.com/articles/247826#1.

58   "Contraceptive Efficacy of Polyester-induce Azoospermia in Normal Men," *Contraception* (1992) https://doi.org/10.1016/0010-7824(92)90157-o.

59   "High Levels of Cycling Training Damage Sperm: What Can Be Done To Protect Triathletes from Infertility?" *Science Daily* https://www.sciencedaily.com/releases/2009/06/090629081755.htm.

60   S.C. Gwynne, *Empire of the Summer Moon: Quanah Parker and the Rise and Fall of the Comanches, the Most Powerful Indian Tribe in American History.* New York: Scribner, 2011.

61   https://doi.org/10.1093/humupd/dmac035.

62   Shanna H. Swan with Stacey Colino, *Count Down: How Our Modern World Is Threatening Sperm Counts, Altering Male and Female Reproductive Development, and Imperiling the Future of the Human Race.* New York: Scribner, 2021.

63   E. Carlsen, A. Giwercman, N. Keiding, and N. E. Skakkebaek, "Evidence for Decreasing Quality of Semen during Past 50 Years," *The British Medical Journal,* September 12, 1992. https://www.bmj.com/content/305/6854/609.

64   Swan, *Count Down,* p. 13.

65   Swan, *Count Down,* p. 13.

66   Robert D. Martin, "Going, Going, Gone? Human Sperm Counts Are Plunging." *Psychology Today,* April 20, 2017. https://www.psychologytoday.com/us/blog/how-we-do-it/201704/going-going-gone-human-sperm-counts-are-plunging.

67   Pallab Ghosh, "Sperm Count Drop 'Could Make Humans Extinct.'" *BBC News,* July 25, 2017. https://www.bbc.com/news/health-40719743.

68   Kashmira Gander, "Household Chemicals Linked to Drop in Male Fertility." *Newsweek,* March 6, 2019. https://www.newsweek.com/male-fertility-scientists-household-chemicals-blame-1353039.

69   Swan, *Count Down,* pp. 27–28.

70   Swan, *Count Down,* pp. 76–77.

71   "Developmental Effects of Endocrine-Disrupting Chemicals in Wildlife and Humans," *Environmental Health Perspectives,* doi.org/10.1289%2Fehp.93101378.

72   "State of the Science of Endocrine Disrupting Chemicals – 2012," https://web.archive.org/web/20130223023915/http://www.who.int/ceh/publications/endocrine/en/index.html.

73   Carson, *Silent Spring* (1962).

74   Swan, *Count Down,* p. 108.

75   Swan, *Count Down,* p. 116.

76   "Prenatal Exposure to Common Plasticizers: a Longitudinal Study on Phthalates, Brain Volumetric Measures, and IQ in Youth," *Nature* (2024), doi.org/10.1038/s41380-023-02225-6.

77   Swan, *Count Down,* p. 118.

78   For example, "Bisphenol S Causes Excessive Estrogen Synthesis by Activating FSHR and the Downstream cAMP/PKA Signaling Pathway," *Communications Biology* (2024), https://doi.org/10.1038/s42003-024-06449-2.

79   "Bisphenol S Induces Brown Adipose Tissue Whitening and Aggravates Diet-induced Obesity in an Estrogen-dependent Manner," *Cell Reports* (2023), https://doi.org/10.1016/j.celrep.2023.113504.

80   "Microplastics: Finding a consensus on the definition," *Marine Pollution Bulletin* (2019), https://doi.org/10.1016/j.marpolbul.2018.11.022.

81   "Effects of the Adsorption Behavior of Polyamide Microplastics on Male Reproductive Health by Reduction of Testosterone Bioavailability," *Ecotoxicology and Environmental Safety* (2024), doi.org/10.1016/j.ecoenv.2023.115747.

82   "Prevalence and Implications of Microplastic Contaminants in General Human Seminal Fluid: A Raman Spectroscopic Study," *Science of the Total Environment* (2024), doi.org/10.1016/j.scitotenv.2024.173522.

83   "Nanoplastics Transport to the Remote, High-Altitude Alps," *Environmental Pollution* (2021), doi.org/10.1016/j.envpol.2021.117697.

84   "First Evidence of Microplastics in Antarctic Snow," *The Cryosphere* (2022), doi.org/10.5194/tc-16-2127-2022, 2022.

85   "Microplastics Affect Mosquito from Aquatic to Terrestrial Lifestyles and Are Transferred to Mammals through Mosquito Bites," *Science of the Total Environment* (2024).

86   "Revealing New Insights: Two-Center Evidence of Microplastics in Human Vitreous Humor and Their Implications for Ocular Health," *Science of the Total Environment* (2024), doi.org/10.1016/j.scitotenv.2024.171109.

87   "Micro- and Nanoplastics Breach the Blood–Brain Barrier (BBB): Biomolecular Corona's Role Revealed," *Nanomaterials* (2023), doi.org/10.3390/nano13081404.

88   "High-Content Screening Discovers Microplastics Released by Contact Lenses under Sunlight," *Environmental Science and Technology* (2023), doi.org/10.3390/nano13081404.

89   "Maternal Exposure to Polystyrene Nanoplastics Causes Defective Retinal Development and Function in Progeny Mice by Disturbing Metabolic Profiles," *Chemosphere* (2024), doi.org/10.1016/j.chemosphere.2024.141513.

90   "Temporal Trends in Sperm Count: a Systematic Review and Meta-regression Analysis of Samples Collected Globally in the 20th and 21st Centuries," *Human Reproduction Update* (2022), https://doi.org/10.1093/humupd/dmac035.

91   Tyrone B. Hayes, Vicky Koury, Anne Narayan, and Sherrie Gallipeau, "Atrazine Induces Complete Feminization and Chemical Castration in Male African Clawed Frogs (Xenopus Laevis) | Proceedings of the National Academy of Sciences." *Proceedings of the National Academy of Sciences of the United States of America.* Accessed December 24, 2024. https://www.pnas.org/doi/full/10.1073/pnas.0909519107.

92   http://dx.doi.org/10.3133/cir1360.

93   Tyrone B. Hayes, et al, "Atrazine Induces Complete Feminization and Chemical Castration in Male African Clawed Frogs (Xenopus Laevis)."

94   Tyrone B. Hayes, et al, "Atrazine Induces Complete Feminization and Chemical Castration in Male African Clawed Frogs (Xenopus Laevis)."

95   T.B. Hayes, A. Collins, M. Lee, M. Mendoza, N. Noriega, A.A. Stuart, and A. Vonk, "Hermaphroditic, demasculinized frogs after exposure to the herbicide atrazine at low ecologically relevant doses." Proc. Natl. Acad. Sci. U.S.A. 99 (8) 5476-5480, https://doi.org/10.1073/pnas.082121499 (2002).

96   Kaufman, "Common Weed Killer Makes Male Frogs Lay Eggs." *National Geographic,* March 2, 2010. https://www.nationalgeographic.com/animals/article/100301-atrazine-frogs-female-chemical.

97   Kaufman, "Common Weed Killer Makes Male Frogs Lay Eggs."

98   "Atrazine." *Atrazine Herbicide.* Accessed December 25, 2024. https://www.atrazine.com/atrazine.

99   An excellent account and discussion here: Lomcz, "If Memes Are Illegal, All Speech Will Become Illegal." *The Federalist,* February 28, 2024. https://thefederalist.com/2024/02/29/if-memes-are-illegal-all-speech-will-become-illegal/. An interview with Mackey can be found here: Tucker Carlson, and Douglass Mackey. "The Douglass Mackey Interview." *The*

Tucker Carlson Network. December, 2023. https://tuckercarlson.com/the-douglass-mackey-interview/.

100 Here it is in all its glory: Alex Jones, "Certified Classic! Gay Frog Thanks Atrazine for Terrible Mutations." *Infowars*, June 2010. https://rumble.com/v35jhku-certified-classic-gay-frog-thanks-atrazine-for-terrible-mutations.html.

101 "White Genocide and Male Extinction in the Rhetoric of Endocrine Disruptors" https://niche-canada.org/2020/06/09/chemical-castration-white-genocide-and-male-extinction-in-rhetoric-of-endocrine-disruption/.

102 Hannah Boast, "Theorizing the Gay Frog," https://doi.org/10.1215/22011919-9962959.

103 "White Genocide and Male Extinction in the Rhetoric of Endocrine Disruptors" https://niche-canada.org/2020/06/09/chemical-castration-white-genocide-and-male-extinction-in-rhetoric-of-endocrine-disruption/.

104 "The mean age of gender dysphoria diagnosis is decreasing" https://doi.org/10.1136/gpsych-2022-100972.

105 "The Amsterdam Cohort of Gender Dysphoria Study (1972–2015): Trends in Prevalence, Treatment, and Regrets," https://doi.org/10.1016/j.jsxm.2018.01.016.

106 "Systematic Review and Meta-Analysis of Prevalence Studies in Transsexualism" https://doi.org/10.1016/j.eurpsy.2015.04.005.

107 Twenge, Jean & Wells, Brooke & Le, Jennifer & Rider, G. Nic. (2024). "Increases in Self-identifying as Transgender Among US Adults," 2014–2022. *Sexuality Research and Social Policy*. 1-19. 10.1007/s13178-024-01001-7.

108 "Validity of the Gender Dysphoria diagnosis and incidence trends in Sweden: a nationwide register study" https://doi.org/10.1038/s41598-021-95421-9.

109 "Parent reports of adolescents and young adults perceived to show signs of a rapid onset of gender dysphoria" https://doi.org/10.1371/journal.pone.0214157.

110 "Comorbidities among Patients with Gender Dysphoria," https://doi.org/10.1155/2014/971814.

111 Raw Egg Nationalist, "The Gay Frogs Election." *The American Mind*, July 13, 2023. https://americanmind.org/salvo/the-gay-frogs-election/.

112 Raw Egg Nationalist, "The Gay Frogs Election." *The American Mind*, July 13, 2023. https://americanmind.org/salvo/the-gay-frogs-election/.

113 Michael Anton, "The Flight 93 Election." *Claremont Review of Books,* September 5, 2016. https://claremontreviewofbooks.com/digital/the-flight-93-election/.

114 John Russell, "RFK Jr. Says Trans Frogs Prove Chemicals in the Water Are Turning Kids Trans." *LGBTQ Nation,* June 22, 2023. https://www.lgbtqnation.com/2023/06/rfk-jr-says-trans-frogs-prove-chemicals-in-the-water-are-turning-kids-trans/.

115 Madeleine Hubbard, "Trump Vows to Create Commission to Probe Chronic Illness Increase, Especially in Kids, If Reelected." *Just The News, June 6, 2023.* https://justthenews.com/politics-policy/all-things-trump/trump-pledges-create-commission-probe-chronic-illness-increase.

116 https://www.minderoo.org/plastic-health-map; "The plastic health map: A systematic evidence map of human health studies on plastic-associated chemicals" https://doi.org/10.1016/j.envint.2023.108225.

117 https://www.asbmb.org/asbmb-today/science/032723/phthalate-alternative-may-harm-brain.

118 "Generally Recognised as Insane," *Valiant News* https://valiantnews.com/2023/12/generally-recognised-as-insane-raw-egg-nationalist/.

119 "The FDA and Moderna's cosy relationship: how lax rules enable a revolving door culture," https://doi.org/10.1136/bmj.p2486.

120 "Is FDA's revolving door open too wide?" https://doi.org/10.1126/science.361.6397.21.

121 "Is FDA's revolving door open too wide?" https://doi.org/10.1126/science.361.6397.21.

122 "The Devil They Knew: Chemical Documents Analysis of Industry Influence on PFAS Science" https://annalsofglobalhealth.org/articles/10.5334/aogh.4013.

123 "Low Perinatal Androgens Predict Recalled Childhood Gender Nonconformity in Men," https://doi.org/10.1177/09567976211036075.

124 "Early Female Transgender Identity After Prenatal Exposure to Diethylstilbestrol: Report from a French National Diethylstilbestrol (DES) Cohort" https://doi.org/10.3390/jox14010010.

125 Raw Egg Nationalist. "Alex Jones Was Right." *American Greatness,* March 2, 2024. https://amgreatness.com/2024/03/01/alex-jones-was-right/.

126 Deepika Kubsad, Eric E. Nilsson, Stephanie E. King, Ingrid Sadler-Riggleman, Daniel Beck, and Michael K. Skinner. "Assessment of Glyphosate Induced Epigenetic Transgenerational Inheritance of Pathologies and Sperm Epimutations: Generational Toxicology." *Nature*

News, April 23, 2019. https://www.nature.com/articles/s41598-019-42860-0.

127 Deepika Kubsad et al, "Assessment of Glyphosate Induced Epigenetic Transgenerational Inheritance of Pathologies and Sperm Epimutations: Generational Toxicology."

128 Deepika Kubsad, et al. "Assessment of Glyphosate Induced Epigenetic Transgenerational Inheritance of Pathologies and Sperm Epimutations: Generational Toxicology."

129 Raw Egg Nationalist, *The Eggs Benedict Option.* Montomery County, PA: Antelope Hill Publishing, 2022.

130 Dan Morgan, *Merchants of Grain* (1979).

131 Morgan, *Merchants of Grain,* p. vii.

132 Morgan, *Merchants of Grain,* p. ix.

133 Morgan, *Merchants of Grain,* p. x.

134 Plato, *Republic,* 59–61. All quotations are taken from these pages. London, Penguin World's Classics edition.

135 Whittaker and Wu, "Low-fat diets and testosterone in men: Systematic review and meta-analysis of intervention studies," *The Journal of Steroid Biochemistry and Molecular Biology* (2021) https://doi.org/10.1016/j.jsbmb.2021.105878.

136 Lambert, "Saturated fat ingestion regulates androgen concentrations and may influence lean body mass accrual," *The Journals of Gerontology. Series A, Biological Sciences and Medical Sciences* (2008) https://doi.org/10.1093/gerona/63.11.1260.

137 EAT Lancet Commission, "EAT - Lancet Commission Summary Report." *EAT Forum,* March 6, 2024. https://eatforum.org/eat-lancet-commission/eat-lancet-commission-summary-report/.

138 EAT Lancet Commission, "EAT - Lancet Commission Summary Report." *EAT.*

139 "Giant Meat and Dairy Companies Are Dominating the Plant-Based and Cellular Meat Market," *Civil Eats* https://civileats.com/2021/09/22/op-ed-giant-meat-and-dairy-companies-are-dominating-the-plant-based-protein-market/.

140 "British Toddlers' Diet Among Worst in World, Experts Warn," *Daily Telegraph.* https://www.telegraph.co.uk/news/2023/02/18/british-toddlers-diet-among-worst-world-experts-warn/.

141 "Ultra-processed food consumption in UK adolescents: distribution, trends, and sociodemographic correlates using the National Diet and Nutrition

Survey 2008/09 to 2018/19," *European Journal of Nutrition* (2024), https://doi.org/10.1007/s00394-024-03458-z.

142 "Microglial cell response to experimental periodontal disease," *Journal of Neuroinflammation* (2023), https://doi.org/10.1186/s12974-023-02821-x.

143 Weston Price, *Nutrition and Physical Degeneration* (1939), chapter 3, "Isolated and Modernized Swiss."

144 Price, *Nutrition and Physical Degeneration*, chapter 12, "Isolated and Modernized New Zealand Maori."

145 Price, *Nutrition and Physical Degeneration*, chapter 9, "Isolated and Modernized African Tribes."

146 Price, *Nutrition and Physical Degeneration*, chapter 16, "Primitive Control of Dental Caries."

147 Price, *Nutrition and Physical Degeneration*, chapter 4, "Isolated and Modernized Gaelics."

148 Grasgruber et al., "Major Correlates of Male Height: A Study of 105 Countries," *Economics and Human Biology* (2016), https://doi.org/10.1016/j.ehb.2016.01.005.

149 Lim et al., "Animal Protein Versus Plant Protein in Supporting Lean Mass and Muscle Strength: A Systematic Review and Meta-Analysis of Randomized Controlled Trials," *Nutrients* (2021), https://doi.org/10.3390%2Fnu13020661.

150 Lim et al., "Animal Protein versus Plant Protein in Supporting Lean Mass and Muscle Strength: A Systematic Review and Meta-Analysis of Randomized Controlled Trials."

151 Gilsing et al., "Serum concentrations of vitamin B12 and folate in British male omnivores, vegetarians and vegans: results from a cross-sectional analysis of the EPIC-Oxford cohort study," *European Journal of Clinical Nutrition* (2010) https://doi.org/10.1038/ejcn.2010.142; Herrmann, "Vitamin B12 Deficiency in vegetarians," *Vegetarian and Plant-Based Diets in Health and Disease Prevention* (2017), https://doi.org/10.1016/B978-0-12-803968-7.00043-5.

152 Hansen et al., "Bone turnover, calcium homeostasis, and vitamin D status in Danish vegans," *European Journal of Clinical Nutrition* (2018), https://doi.org/10.1038/s41430-017-0081-y; Igaucel et al. "Veganism, vegetarianism, bone mineral density, and fracture risk: a systematic review and meta-analysis," *Nutrition Reviews* (2019), https://doi.org/10.1093/nutrit/nuy045.

153 Malcolm Kendrick. *The Great Cholesterol Con: The Truth about What Really Causes Heart Disease and How to Avoid It*. London: John Blake, 2008.

154 Catherine Shanahan with Luke Shanahan, *Deep Nutrition: Why Your Genes Need Traditional Food*. New York: Flatiron Books, 2017.

155 "The U.S. government is poised to withdraw longstanding warnings about cholesterol," *Washington Post,* https://www.washingtonpost.com/news/wonk/wp/2015/02/10/feds-poised-to-withdraw-longstanding-warnings-about-dietary-cholesterol/.

156 Ramsden et al., "Re-evaluation of the traditional diet-heart hypothesis: analysis of recovered data from Minnesota Coronary Experiment (1968-73)," *British Medical Journal* (2016), https://doi.org/10.1136/bmj.i1246.

157 Tuikkala et al., "Serum total cholesterol levels and all-cause mortality in a home-dwelling elderly population: a six-year follow-up," *Scandinavian Journal of Primary Health Care* (2010), https://doi.org/10.3109/02813432.2010.487371.

158 Yi et al., "Total cholesterol and all-cause mortality by sex and age: a prospective cohort study among 12.8 million adults," *Scientific Reports* (2019), https://doi.org/10.1038/s41598-018-38461-y.

159 Zureik et al., "Decline in serum total cholesterol and the risk of death from cancer," *Epidemiology* (1997) doi.org/10.1097/00001648-199703000-00003.

160 Mamounis et al., "Linoleic acid causes greater weight gain than saturated fat without hypothalamic inflammation in the male mouse," *The Journal of nutritional biochemistry* (2017), https://doi.org/10.1016/j.jnutbio.2016.10.016.

161 Deol et al., "Dysregulation of Hypothalamic Gene Expression and the Oxytocinergic System by Soybean Oil Diets in Male Mice," *Endocrinology* (2020), https://doi.org/10.1210/endocr/bqz044.

162 Deol et al., "Dysregulation of Hypothalamic Gene Expression and the Oxytocinergic System by Soybean Oil Diets in Male Mice."

163 On the "soyboy" conspiracy theory, see, for instance, "Inside the 'soy boy' conspiracy theory: It combines misogyny and the warped world of pseudoscience," *Salon,* https://www.salon.com/2018/11/14/the-soy-boy-conspiracy-theory-alt-right-thinks-left-wing-has-it-out-for-them-with-soybeans_partner/.

164 See, for example, Reed et al., "Neither soy nor isoflavone intake affects male reproductive hormones: An expanded and updated meta-analysis of clinical studies," *Reproductive Toxicology* (2021), https://doi.org/10.1016/j.reprotox.2020.12.019.

165 Nishikawa et al., "Secondary Hypogonadism due to Excessive Ingestion of Isoflavone in a Man," *Internal Medicine* (Tokyo, Japan) (2022), https://doi.org/10.2169/internalmedicine.8578-21.

166 Richard Florida, *The Great Reset,* p. 5.

167 James C. Scott, *Against the Grain.*

168 Raw Egg Nationalist, *The Eggs Benedict Option,* p. 55. My account of the deficits of the Agricultural Revolution is taken from pages 55–67.

169 Allentoft et al. "Population Genomics of Stone Age Eurasia," (doi. org/10.1101/2022.05.04.490594). This paper was subsequently published in *Nature,* in 2024, as "Population Genomics of Post-Glacial Western Eurasia."

170 James C. Scott, *Against the Grain,* pp. 219–56.

171 Scott, *Against the Grain,* p. 217.

172 "Let them eat steak: Emergency stocks of meat and eggs flown into Paris Olympic village," *The Australian.*

173 "It Turns Out 3/4 of Men Would Rather Die Young Than Give Up Meat," *Men's Health,* https://www.menshealth.com/uk/nutrition/a36261605/red-meat-health/.

174 "Europe Plant-Based Food Market Worth $16.70 Billion by 2029," https://www.meticulousresearch.com/pressrelease/484/europe-plant-based-food-market-2029?utm_source=Globnewswire&utm_medium=Paid&utm_campaign=Product&utm_content=30-03-2022.

175 Parkin and Atwood, "Menu Design Approaches to Promote Sustainable Vegetarian Food Choices When Dining Out," *Journal of Environmental Psychology,* https://doi.org/10.1016/j.jenvp.2021.101721.

176 Ye and Mattila, "The Effect of Ad Appeals and Message Framing on Consumer Responses to Plant-Based Menu Items," *International Journal of Hospitality Management,* https://doi.org/10.1016/j.ijhm.2021.102917.

177 "You Want to Buy Meat? In This Economy?" *The New York Times,* https://www.nytimes.com/2022/06/02/opinion/inflation-vegetarian-vegan.html.

178 "'We Will Save Our Beef': Florida Bans Lab-Grown Meat," *The New York Times,* https://www.nytimes.com/2024/05/03/climate/florida-lab-grown-meat-ban.html.

179 "Governor DeSantis Signs Legislation to Keep Lab-Grown Meat Out of Florida," https://www.flgov.com/2024/05/01/governor-desantis-signs-legislation-to-keep-lab-grown-meat-out-of-florida/.

180 Gea et al., "Can oestrogenic activity in air contribute to the overall body burden of endocrine disruptors?" *Environmental Toxicology and Pharmacology* (2023), https://doi.org/10.1016/j.etap.2023.104232.

181 Zhang et al., "Occurrence of Polyethylene Terephthalate and Polycarbonate Microplastics in Infant and Adult Feces,"

Environmental Science and Technology Letters 8:11 (2021), https://doi
.org/10.1021/acs.estlett.1c00559.

182 Yadav et al., "Cutting Boards: An Overlooked Source of Microplastics
in Human Food?" *Environmental Science and Technology* 57:22
(2023), https://doi.org/10.1021/acs.est.3c00924.

183 He et al., "Migration of (non-) intentionally added substances
and microplastics from microwavable plastic food containers,"
Journal of Hazardous Materials 417:5 (2021), https://doi.org/10
.1016/j.jhazmat.2021.126074.

184 Hyland et al., "Urinary Glyphosate Concentrations among
Pregnant Participants in a Randomized, Crossover Trial of Organic
and Conventional Diets," *Environmental Health Perspectives*
(2023), https://doi.org/10.1289/EHP12155.

185 "100% of Top Twenty Fast Food Brands Positive for Glyphosate Herbicide
76% Positive for Harmful Pesticides," https://www.momsacrossamerica.
com/fast_food_glyphosate_herbicide.

186 See, for instance, Nguyen and Powell, "The Impact of
Restaurant Consumption among US Adults: Effects on
Energy and Nutrient Intakes," *Public Health Nutrition* 17:11
(2014), https://doi.org/10.1017/S1368980014001153.

187 Luo et al., "Raman Imaging for the Identification of Teflon
Microplastics and Nanoplastics Released from Non-
stick Cookware," *Science of the Total Environment* 851:2
(2022), https://doi.org/10.1016/j.scitotenv.2022.158293.

188 "We sampled tap water across the US—and found arsenic, lead and toxic
chemicals," www.theguardian.com/us-news/2021/mar/31/americas-tap-
water-samples-forever-chemicals.

189 Hart et al., "A Characterization of Personal Care Product Use among
Undergraduate Female College Students in South Carolina, USA,"
Journal of Exposure Science and Environmental Epidemiology, 30:1
(2020), https://doi.org/10.1038/s41370-019-0170-1.

190 Harley et al., "Reducing Phthalate, Paraben, and Phenol Exposure
from Personal Care Products in Adolescent Girls: Findings from the
HERMOSA Intervention Study," *Environmental Health Perspectives*
124:10 (2016), https://doi.org/10.1289/ehp.1510514.

191 Genuis et al., "Human Elimination of Phthalate Compounds:
Blood, Urine and Sweat (BUS) Study," *Scientific World Journal*
(2012), https://doi.org/10.1100/2012/615068.

192 Ross and Sternquist, "Methamphetamine exposure and chronic
illness in police officers: significant improvement with sauna-based

detoxification therapy," *Toxicology and Industrial Health* 28:8 (2012), https://doi.org/10.1177/0748233711425070.

193 Jandacek and Tso, "Factors Affecting the Storage and Excretion of Toxic Lipophilic Xenobiotics," *Lipids* 36:12 (2001), https://doi.org/10.1007/s11745-001-0844-z.

194 Gasiorowski et al., "Effect of Plasma and Blood Donations on Levels of Perfluoroalkyl and Polyfluoroalkyl Substances in Firefighters in Australia: A Randomized Clinical Trial," *JAMA Network Open* 5:4 (2022), doi.org/10.1001/jamanetworkopen.2022.6257.

195 Lorber et al., "The Effect of Ongoing Blood Loss on Human Serum Concentrations of Perfluorinated Acids," *Chemosphere* 118 (2015), https://doi.org/10.1016/j.chemosphere.2014.07.093.

196 Håkonsen et al., "Does Weight Loss Improve Semen Quality and Reproductive Hormones? Results from a Cohort of Severely Obese Men," *Reproductive Health* 8 (2011), https://doi.org/10.1186/1742-4755-8-24.

197 Smith et al., "Examining the Effects of Calorie Restriction on Testosterone Concentrations in Men: a Systematic Review and Meta-analysis," *Nutrition Reviews* 80:5 (2022), https://doi.org/10.1093/nutrit/nuab072.

198 Kumagai et al., "Lifestyle Modification Increases Serum Testosterone Level and Decrease [sic] Central Blood Pressure in Overweight and Obese Men," *Endocrine Journal* 62: 5 (2015), https://doi.org/10.1507/endocrj.EJ14-0555.

199 "The Race Is on To Stop Ozempic Muscle Loss," *The New York Times* https://www.nytimes.com/2024/02/08/well/live/ozempic-muscle-loss-exercise.html.

200 Lisco et al., "Glucagon-like peptide 1 receptor agonists and thyroid cancer: is it the time to be concerned?" *Endocrine Connections* 12:11 (2023), https://doi.org/10.1530/EC-23-0257.

201 McDermott et al., "Molecular-Level Dysregulation of Insulin Pathways and Inflammatory Processes in Peripheral Blood Mononuclear Cells by Circadian Misalignment," *Journal of Proteome Research* 23:5 (2024), https://doi.org/10.1021/acs.jproteome.3c00418.

202 Marquezea et al., "Weight Gain in Relation to Night Work among Nurses," *Work* 41:1 (2012), https://doi.org/10.3233/WOR-2012-0429-2043 and Streng et al., "Night Shift Work Characteristics Are Associated with Several Elevated Metabolic Risk Factors and Immune Cell Counts in a Cross-sectional Study," *Scientific Reports* 12 (2022), https://doi.org/10.1038/s41598-022-06122-w.

203 Patel et al., "Association between Reduced Sleep and Weight Gain in Women," *American Journal of Epidemiology*, 164:10 (2006), https://doi.org/10.1093/aje/kwj280.

204 Scott et al., "Are We Getting Enough Sleep? Frequent Irregular Sleep Found in an Analysis of over 11 Million Nights of Objective In-home Sleep Data," *Sleep Health* 10:1 (2024), https://doi.org/10.1016/j.sleh.2023.10.016.

205 Su et al., "Effect of Partial and Total Sleep Deprivation on Serum Testosterone in Healthy Males: A Systematic Review and Meta-Analysis," *Sleep Medicine* 88 (2021), https://doi.org/10.1016/j.sleep.2021.10.031.

206 Leproult and Coulter, "Effect of 1 Week of Sleep Restriction on Testosterone Levels in Young Healthy Men," *Journal of the American Medical Association* 305:21 (2011), doi.org/10.1001/jama.2011.710.

207 Penev, "Association between Sleep and Morning Testosterone Levels in Older Men," *Sleep* 30:4 (2007), https://doi.org/10.1093/sleep/30.4.427.

208 Dauchy et al., "Circadian and Melatonin Disruption by Exposure to Light at Night Drives Intrinsic Resistance to Tamoxifen Therapy in Breast Cancer," *Cancer Research* 74:15 (2014), https://doi.org/10.1158/0008-5472.CAN-13-3156.

209 Chottanapund et al., "Anti-aromatase Effect of Resveratrol and Melatonin on Hormonal Positive Breast Cancer Cells Co-cultured with Breast Adipose Fibroblasts," *Toxicology in Vitro* 28: 7 (2014), https://doi.org/10.1016/j.tiv.2014.05.015.

210 Goh and Tong, "Sleep, Sex Steroids, Sexual Activities, and Aging in Asian Men," *Journal of Andrology* 31:2 (2010), https://doi.org/10.2164/jandrol.109.007856.

211 Haghayegh et al., "Before-bedtime passive body heating by warm shower or bath to improve sleep: A systematic review and meta-analysis," *Sleep Medicine Reviews* 46 (2019), https://doi.org/10.1016/j.smrv.2019.04.008.

212 Lee et al., "Effects of Exercise with or without Light Exposure on Sleep Quality and Hormone Responses," *Journal of Exercise Nutrition and Biochemistry* 18:3 (2014), https://doi.org/10.5717/jenb.2014.18.3.293.

213 Chris Wright, "The Great Biohack: Inside the broad, sometimes bizarre world of human augmentation," *Wired*, https://wired.me/technology/the-great-biohack-future-human-performance.

214 Joel Snape, "'My ultimate goal? Don't die': Bryan Johnson on his controversial plan to live for ever," *The Guardian* (2023), https://www.theguardian.com/society/2023/sep/14/my-ultimate-goal-dont-die-bryan-johnson-on-his-controversial-plan-to-live-for-ever.

215 Bryan Johnson, "I Did Gene Therapy on a Secret Island," https://x.com/bryan_johnson/status/1803105493281546566.

216 "Ecce Homos," *American Mind,* https://americanmind.org/salvo/ecce-homos/.

217 Aristotle, *The Politics,* Bk. V, Ch. 11.

218 C.A. Forbes, "Expanded Uses of the Greek Gymnasium," *Classical Philology 40:1* (1945), p. 33.

219 N.B. Crowther, "Slaves and Greek Athletics," *Quaderni Urbinati di Cultura Classica,* New Ser. 40:1 (1992), pp. 35–43.

220 Katherine Viner, "Snipped in Solidarity: The American Men Getting Vasectomies after Roe – While They Can." *The Guardian,* July 28, 2022. https://www.theguardian.com/us-news/2022/jul/27/vasectomy-roe-v-wade-abortion-supreme-court.

221 Katherine Viner, "Snipped in Solidarity: The American Men Getting Vasectomies after Roe – While They Can."

222 "Scientists Are on the Verge of a Male Birth-control Pill. Will Men Take It?" *The Guardian,* https://www.theguardian.com/commentisfree/2023/dec/18/male-birth-control-will-men-take-it.

223 Wang et al., "Male Hormonal Contraception : Where Are We Now?" *Current Obstetrics and Gynecology Reports 29:5* (2016), https://doi.org/10.1007/s13669-016-0140-8.

224 Reynolds-Wright et al., "Will Men Use Novel Male Contraceptive Methods and Will Women Trust Them? A Systematic Review," *The Journal of Sex Research* 58:7 (2021), https://doi.org/10.1080/00224499.2021.1905764.

225 "Two Versions of Masculinity Are on the 2024 Ballot," *Axios,* https://www.axios.com/2024/08/24/walz-trump-emhoff-masculinity-fatherhood.

226 Many of Peat's essays can be read at raypeat.com. I would recommend the essay, "The Dark Side of Stress (Learned Helplessness)."

227 Zak, "Testosterone Administration Induces a Red Shift in Democrats," https://doi.org/10.3886/E155441V1.

228 Kierkegaard, "Mental Illness and the Left," *Mankind Quarterly* 65:1 (2024), http://doi.org/10.46469/mq.2020.60.4.3.

229 Napier et al., "Why Are Conservatives Happier than Liberals?" *Psychological Science* 19:6 (2008), https://doi.org/10.1111/j.1467-9280.2008.02124.x.

230 Burton et al., "Why Do Conservatives Report Being Happier than Liberals? The Contribution of Neuroticism," *Journal of Social and Political Psychology* 3:1 (2015), https://doi.org/10.5964/jspp.v3i1.117.

231 Liao et al., "Testosterone Administration Modulates Inequality Aversion in Healthy Males: Evidence from Computational Modeling,"

Psychoneuroendocrinology 155: 106321 (2023), https://doi.org/10
.1016/j.psyneuen.2023.106321.

232 Inoue et al., "Testosterone Promotes Either Dominance or Submissiveness
in the Ultimatum Game Depending on Players' Social Rank," *Scientific
Reports* 13,7:5335 (2017), https://doi.org/10.1038/s41598-017-05603-7.

233 Riemers and Diekhof, "Testosterone Is Associated with
Cooperation during Intergroup Competition by Enhancing
Parochial Altruism," *Frontiers in Neuroscience* 12, 9:183
(2015), doi.org/10.3389/fnins.2015.00183.

234 Muñoz-Reyes et al., "The Male Warrior Hypothesis:
Testosterone-related Cooperation and Aggression in the
Context of Intergroup Conflict," *Scientific Reports* 10,1:375
(2020), doi.org/10.1038/s41598-019-57259-0.

235 Kanai et al., "Political Orientations Are Correlated with Brain Structure
in Young Adults," *Current Biology* 21:8 (2011), https://doi.org
/10.1016/j.cub.2011.03.017.

236 Radke et al., "Testosterone Biases the Amygdala Toward Social
Threat Approach," *Science Advances* 1:5 (2015), https://doi.org
/10.1126/sciadv.1400074.

237 Brouillard et al., "Morphologic Alterations of the Fear Circuitry:
The Role of Sex Hormones and Oral Contraceptives," *Frontiers in
Endocrinology* 14 (2023), https://doi.org/10.3389/fendo.2023.1228504.

238 Johansson et al., "Population-based Cohort Study of Oral Contraceptive
Use and Risk of Depression," *Epidemiology and Psychiatric Sciences* 32
(2023), https://doi.org/10.1017/S2045796023000525.

239 See, for example, "Why Have Women Become Left Wing? The Political
Gender Gap and the Decline in Marriage," *Quarterly Journal of
Economics* 117:3 (2002). More recently, much ink has been spilled
on the topic of "women's leftward expansion," as Gallup put it, with
emphasis placed on the effects of the Trump presidency and the repeal
of Roe v. Wade, but as I say this is a phenomenon observed across the
Developed World, not just in the U.S.

240 James, "The Moral Equivalent of War."

241 James, "The Moral Equivalent of War."

242 Sigmund Freud, *Civilization and Its Discontents,* London: Penguin, 2002,
chapter 8.

243 Fukuyama, *The End of History and the Last Man,* p. 329.

244 Fukuyama, *The End of History and the Last Man,* p. 336.